THE POACHER'S NIGHTMARE

THE POACHER'S NIGHTMARE

Stories of an Undercover Game Warden

KENNIE PRINCE

Edited by James L. Cummins

Foreword by Alfred Nicols

University Press of Mississippi / Jackson

Wildlife Mississippi

Publication of this book was made possible in part
by a generous donation from Wildlife Mississippi.

The University Press of Mississippi is the scholarly publishing agency of the
Mississippi Institutions of Higher Learning: Alcorn State University, Delta State
University, Jackson State University, Mississippi State University, Mississippi
University for Women, Mississippi Valley State University, University of
Mississippi, and University of Southern Mississippi.

www.upress.state.ms.us

The University Press of Mississippi is a member
of the Association of University Presses.

This work depicts actual events in the life of the author. The names and identifying
details of some individuals have been changed to protect their privacy.

Photographs courtesy of the author unless otherwise noted.

Copyright © 2023 by University Press of Mississippi
All rights reserved
Manufactured in the United States of America

First printing 2023

∞

Library of Congress Cataloging-in-Publication Data

Names: Prince, Kennie, author. | Cummins, James L., Jr., 1965– editor,
writer of preface. | Nicols, Alfred (Alfred G.) Jr., writer of foreword.
Title: The poacher's nightmare : stories of an undercover game warden /
Kennie Prince; edited by James L. Cummins; foreword by Alfred Nicols.
Description: Jackson : University Press of Mississippi, 2023.
Identifiers: LCCN 2023019863 (print) | LCCN 2023019864 (ebook) | ISBN
9781496846891 (hardcover) | ISBN 9781496850317 (trade paperback) | ISBN
9781496846907 (epub) | ISBN 9781496846914 (epub) |
ISBN 9781496846921 (pdf) | ISBN 9781496846938 (pdf)
Subjects: LCSH: Prince, Kennie. | Undercover wildlife
agents—Mississippi—Biography. | Game wardens—Mississippi—Biography.
| Poaching—Mississippi. | Hunters—Mississippi—Anecdotes. | Wildlife
management—Mississippi—Anecdotes. | Wildlife
crimes—Mississippi—Anecdotes. | Wildlife
conservation—Mississippi—Anecdotes.
Classification: LCC SK354.P75 A3 2023 (print) | LCC SK354.P75 (ebook) |
DDC 333.95/41709762—dc23/eng/20230605
LC record available at https://lccn.loc.gov/2023019863
LC ebook record available at https://lccn.loc.gov/2023019864

British Library Cataloging-in-Publication Data available

CONTENTS

Foreword — vii

Editor's Note — xi

Preface — xv

CHAPTER 1 — A Game Warden in the Making — 3

CHAPTER 2 — The Job of a Lifetime — 9

CHAPTER 3 — Law Enforcement: Never a Dull Day! — 19

CHAPTER 4 — You're Late! A Dove Case Resulted in a Friendship — 33

CHAPTER 5 — Ducks in the Darkness: Where's Bob? — 37

CHAPTER 6 — The Real Quack! — 43

CHAPTER 7 — Chasing a Friend: Illegal Nets — 45

CHAPTER 8 — High-Speed Headlighters — 49

CHAPTER 9 — Officer under Fire! — 53

CHAPTER 10 — Going Under: Transferring to Special Ops — 57

CHAPTER 11 — Chasing Home Boys in the Bitterroot Mountains — 61

CHAPTER 12 — The Big One: Operation Cold Storage — 73

CHAPTER 13 — Turtles Going to China! — 93

CHAPTER 14 — Deer, Dope, and Beer: Operation Triangle — 97

Contents

CHAPTER 15 — Operation AST: Lacey Act Violations — 105

CHAPTER 16 — Sweet Victory: The Carrollton Zoo — 109

CHAPTER 17 — Crappie and Whitetails along the Mississippi River: Operation Delta — 115

CHAPTER 18 — Duck Mercenary — 123

CHAPTER 19 — Muddy Caviar — 129

CHAPTER 20 — Hot and Fully Automatic: Operation Rooster — 137

CHAPTER 21 — Black Market Bucks — 149

CHAPTER 22 — Wild Turkeys for Sale — 153

CHAPTER 23 — Duck Hunt with My Dentist — 155

CHAPTER 24 — Champion Trap Shooter! — 157

CHAPTER 25 — Operation Stoned Duck, My Last Op — 163

Author's Note — 181

Acknowledgments — 185

FOREWORD

My friend Kennie Prince is a living legend. He is a skilled outdoorsman and game warden who has dedicated his life to the protection of Mississippi's fish and wildlife resources. Now, at the urging of so many of his friends and colleagues, he has written a compelling memoir about his long and unparalleled career as a covert wildlife agent, infiltrating the criminal element and gaining their trust; then, involving other state and federal law enforcement officials, bringing an abrupt and painful halt to their criminal activities such as stealing vast fish and wildlife resources from the public trust. Smart, creative, knowledgeable, tenacious, disciplined, and passionate, and a natural actor, Kennie has a unique set of qualities that made him a perfect fit for this dangerous undertaking.

Kennie first came to my attention when I was a state circuit judge in Rankin and Madison Counties in Mississippi, where he served as a young game warden. With my criminal docket being filled with major felonies, game violations were generally handled by the lower courts. But Kennie was often talked about around the courthouse as the person who could catch the crafty violators that others couldn't catch—those violating laws from headlighting deer to trespassing, to hunting migratory birds over bait, to illegally gill-netting fish on the Ross Barnett Reservoir, to exceeding the legal limits of almost every activity. His job had no set hours; his stamina and willingness to "suffer for the resource" had no limits. He was even the person who could charm the largest nuisance alligator into being caught when others couldn't get close to it.

But when Kennie's unique qualities and talents most came to my attention was when I left the state circuit judge position to accept an appointment as a US magistrate judge for the Southern District of Mississippi. In this role, I was a frequent judicial participant in many of the cases Kennie mentions in this memoir, often in contact with Kennie, US Fish and Wildlife Service Special Agent Robert Oliveri, and Assistant US Attorney John Dowdy. They were in my office on a regular basis at this time seeking warrants and obtaining settings for trials and pleas. Oliveri and Dowdy were in awe at what Kennie could do with the assignments given to him.

Throughout the course of this memoir, Kennie relates dozens of captivating stories of covert wildlife operations, often spanning years and requiring ingenious planning, challenging secrecy, and careful coordination. As his reputation for unparalleled success grew in national wildlife law enforcement circles, many of these cases involved him agreeing to accept covert assignments in other states, as far away as Idaho and North Dakota. Tight-knit circles of loyal and suspicious criminals are hard to penetrate, but Kennie had what it took to gain their confidence. A man of Kennie Prince's acting ability, broad knowledge, and dedication is hard to find, and he was in constant demand.

Among the many intriguing cases covered in this memoir is the famous Operation Cold Storage. This operation was conceived by Kennie and was the largest covert wildlife operation in the history of the State of Mississippi. It lasted for almost two years and resulted in approximately 140 individuals being charged and convicted in Mississippi and Louisiana of numerous wildlife violations, felony violations of the Lacey Act, and numerous violations of felony firearms and narcotics laws. This operation helped garner a national award for the Mississippi covert operations team and was the subject of a feature on the Discovery Channel.

Apart from his legendary career in wildlife law enforcement, Kennie is a remarkable man, outstanding in so many other ways. Having a lifelong interest in martial arts, he is accomplished in many styles and has taught defensive tactics at the Mississippi Law Enforcement Training Academy, as well as privately. He is an accomplished bowhunter and trapper, being a lifetime member of the Mississippi Bowhunters Association and the Mississippi Trappers Association.

Kennie starting trapping at the age of eight and, since retiring in 2009, has become Mississippi's foremost trapper, trapping nuisance animals such as beavers, wild hogs, coyotes, and alligators and catching dangerous, poisonous snakes, not only in Mississippi but in many other areas of the country. Always one to share his knowledge, he has taken leadership roles in local and national trappers' associations and has taught trapping at workshops locally and across the country. He even taught me to trap coyotes on my rural land in Copiah County, Mississippi. Watching him make and set coyote traps is awesome! He can dig the hole; stake, bait, and set the trap; and cover and camouflage it in not much more time than it takes me to brush my teeth. He has even designed a state-of-the-art hog trap, which was featured in *Wildlife Mississippi* magazine. One I got from him caught thirteen wild hogs in one night!

Kennie lives with his wife Betty in Rankin County, Mississippi. A committed Christian, he is active in his church and in other religious endeavors. A devoted family man, he has four children with Betty and six grandchildren, all giving him great pride. I am blessed to have him as a longtime friend, and honored to have this part in introducing readers to Kennie's engrossing memoir about his life and commitment to protecting the wild places and wild things that make our state and nation so great.

—Alfred Nicols

EDITOR'S NOTE

In colonial America, there were few regulations about fish and wildlife. Our founders had the vision to set up a system of fish and wildlife conservation, and hunting and fishing, that was vastly different from what had existed in England and other countries where the early settlers came from. There, monarchs owned the fish and wildlife and the rights to take them. Early in our nation's history, our Supreme Court ruled that this "property" that had once belonged to the monarch was now owned by the people—and equally—to be held in the public trust. This eventually led to our current system of hunting and fishing, and the North American model of wildlife conservation.

However, people were free to kill and sell fish and wildlife, resulting in a major decline in populations. Our nation, including Mississippi, lost the passenger pigeon, for example. In the 1930s, the white-tailed deer population in Mississippi dwindled to approximately 1,500 animals, compared to approximately 1.5 million today.

Concerned hunters took notice. In 1887, Theodore Roosevelt and others started the Boone and Crockett Club—conserving big game and furthering policy for those purposes were its main tasks. It is North America's oldest conservation organization, and I am fortunate to serve as its current president. Theodore Roosevelt was its first. The club saw a crisis in humanity's impact on wildlife and their habitats and called citizens to action to change America's direction. Roosevelt and others, including several dedicated Mississippians—L. Q. C. Lamar, Key Pittman, and Fannye Cook, to name a few—led the way toward creating a system of conservation that is now the envy of the world.

These early leaders in the conservation movement initially focused on protecting wild places and impeding the killing of fish and wildlife for markets. They shaped the conservation policies of North America and developed the cornerstones of the conservation movement, including: the creation and establishment of the National Forest system, the National Park system, the

National Wildlife Refuge system, and the federal agencies to oversee them; the establishment of modern-day game laws such as hunting seasons and bag limits to allow taking while sustaining fish and wildlife populations; and the promotion of ethical hunting of wildlife through concepts of fair chase—which made the national news in 1902 when Roosevelt and Holt Collier hunted black bear in the vast swamps of the Mississippi Delta and Roosevelt refused to shoot a defenseless bear.

Not only is conserving wild places and wild things important, but how we pursue wildlife, like when Roosevelt set the example with the bear in Sharkey County, is equally important. Wildlife must be given the chance of escape— that's called fair chase.

As hunters, we must always remember that fish and wildlife belong to the people and that hunting and fishing is a privilege. How people view these activities will determine their future. Jim Posewitz, in his book *Beyond Fair Chase*, defines an ethical hunter as "a person who knows and respects the animals hunted, follows the law, and behaves in a way that will satisfy what society expects of him or her as hunter." Unfortunately, there are many smart people today who say that hunting should end. Poachers and other unethical hunters are giving hunting a bad name and are jeopardizing hunting's future existence.

I have known Kennie Prince for more than forty years. He understands that taking care of the fish and wildlife resources that God has given us is a great moral responsibility. And that how hunters and anglers are perceived will determine the future of hunting and fishing. In fact, he has dedicated his life to making sure that future generations of Mississippians will have the same opportunities to enjoy them as he, I, and many other Mississippians have.

This book is a compelling memoir about Kennie's career as a covert wildlife agent. It is intended for those people who will either choose to do right with our natural resources, pursue a career conserving them, or are just curious about what a covert wildlife agent does. Wildlife Mississippi is truly honored to underwrite the publication of this book. Conservation officers—especially those who go undercover—risk their lives to make sure the rest of society has an opportunity to enjoy our natural resources. The work of undercover conservation officers—especially that of Kennie—is unknown to most Mississippians, and this great book will help all of us get to know him and their work a little better. And, hopefully, have a lot more respect for them.

Wildlife Mississippi has made notable progress in conserving the state's natural resources since we were formed twenty-five years ago by protecting, restoring, and enhancing over six hundred thousand acres of land in the state. We haven't done it alone but by working with a community of like-minded people, private landowners, other organizations, and government agencies. We believe that a clean environment and functioning natural systems can help make our economy healthy. Wildlife Mississippi's vision statement is: "The conservation of Mississippi's lands, waters, and natural heritage will secure the state's quality of life by making it a better place to live, work, and raise a family."

Nowhere is that linkage more apparent than in the Mississippi Delta, where Wildlife Mississippi began working over two decades ago, in the late 1990s—and where Kennie has spent a lot of time. There, groundwater is being withdrawn for irrigation faster than it can be replenished. No less than the future of the one of the world's richest agricultural economies is at stake.

And, with 80 percent of Americans now living in urban areas—and farther from natural spaces—our challenge is to help people maintain enough of a connection to the land and the natural world to care about it and see it as essential to their well-being. Hunting and fishing is a part of this as well.

Thanks to Kennie and other conservation officers—and those who have dedicated their life to conserving Mississippi's wild places and wild things—there are still places in our great state where nature is within reach and holding its ground. Horn Island, part of what is now the Gulf Islands National Seashore, is about as wild as any place in America. The bottomland hardwood forests of the Mississippi River floodplain, although hidden behind levees that stretch longer than the Great Wall of China, cover more than a million acres in Mississippi and neighboring states. The many two-thousand-year-old, giant bald cypress trees of Sky Lake rival the giant sequoias and redwoods of California. Rivers such as the Pascagoula, Pearl, Buttahatchie, and Bayou Pierre still harbor ancient species such as Gulf sturgeon, walleye, alligator gar, and paddlefish as well as turtles, fish, and mussels found nowhere else in the world.

Wildlife Mississippi is working in all these places and more. It is even developing opportunities for Mississippians to discover and learn about the natural world close to home, such as the Fannye Cook Natural Area in the heart of the Jackson metropolitan area. This three-thousand-acre tract along the Pearl River in Flowood, the first natural area to be named for Mississippi's founding conservationist, Fannye Cook, will be used for conservation education, walking, biking, paddling, nature photography, hunting, fishing, and other activities—something we think Ms. Cook would be proud of. More than eight hundred thousand people live within an hour's drive of this area—Mississippi's largest urban, natural area.

Thankfully, many Mississippians value outdoor experiences, perhaps more than the people of almost any other state—something famed conservationist Aldo Leopold recognized almost one hundred years ago. Today, more Mississippians care about healthy fish and wildlife populations and functioning natural systems than at any other time in our state's history. They believe, as

Kennie and James bowfishing on Ross Barnett in 1984. Photo by David Watts.

Wildlife Mississippi does, that all of us share a responsibility to conserve them for present and future generations. Our approach is to help people, especially private landowners, see that conservation often makes common sense *and* economic sense. We do that by working with government agencies, policy leaders, and businesses to create incentives to protect water quality and conserve natural habitats.

Wildlife Mississippi believes that it is not enough to preach that all of us have an unquestionable responsibility to conserve the fish and wildlife resources around us; we must practice it, too. This includes regulated hunting and fishing. But by no means does it include the illegal and senseless taking of our natural resources. Posewitz also said, "A society or culture is ultimately measured not by what it develops or consumes, but rather by what it has nurtured and preserved." That's what Kennie Prince has done through his selfless and steadfast actions to make Mississippi a better place to live, work, and raise a family by preventing a few "bad apples" from stealing from the public trust.

We can all do our job to conserve the state's natural resources, but it takes people like Kennie to protect them.

To learn more about Wildlife Mississippi's work, see www.wildlifemiss.org.

—James L. Cummins

PREFACE

In 1983, I began my career with the Mississippi Department of Wildlife Conservation as a fisheries technician. It was in 1986 that I became a game warden. I have shared many of the stories of my career with a lot of people at various speaking events. Many times, folks would say, "You need to write a book." Well, after three years of pecking out some of my memories of the many experiences I had while working for the agency, and a lot of encouragement from a lot of folks, it has finally come together. The stories I have written are from on-the-job experiences. From the fisheries division and the game division, where I did nuisance alligator work, to the goal of having a career in law enforcement—I went from being a uniformed game warden to spending my last years in special operations doing undercover work—it has been a joyous adventure.

I was fortunate to have been raised in a time with no cell phones, no internet, and only three channels on television. Growing up, I spent most of my time playing in the woods and creeks near my home. My father spent lots of time with me, taking me hunting and fishing every chance he had. Most of all, he also taught me about good work ethics and working hard. He taught me that taking care of your family comes first, with God being the center of it all. I see a lot of people today with these priorities out of order, or being too obsessive about one thing or another.

My mother also spent time with me and my siblings, riding horses and participating in other outdoor activities. She would take us, on our horses, to Pelahatchie Creek for swimming. We would water-ski while she drove the boat. She even took us fishing on many Saturdays. She wasn't a "stay inside, television watcher," type of woman, so I attribute her life as well to my love of the outdoors. Our family was in church on Sundays; it was a regular and important part of our life, too. I truly thank God for my parents, who were both stern and served as great examples of how I should live my life.

I grew up loving the outdoors! There wasn't anything that I didn't hunt—deer, turkeys, rabbits, squirrels, doves, and ducks. In the springtime after turkey season ended, I would be on Pelahatchie Creek or the Pearl River running trotlines, fishing, and chasing gators. In 1968, I caught my first beaver with a trap, and to this day, after my retirement, I'm trapping full-time for beavers and predators. One might say I love to catch things—from wildlife to people—so much so that I made a life out of it! I hope that until God calls me home, I'm able to continue doing what I love to do, but a lot less on the people-catching side of things. Never would I have imagined that I would spend a life getting paid for "living the dream."

God opened doors in my life that made me who I am. My dreams in life as a teenager were to go to the Rocky Mountains and be a mountain man. At age seventeen, at a bow-hunting convention, I met a man named Doug King who owned a guiding operation in Colorado. I sold my deer rifle to get a plane ticket to go on a bow hunt for mule deer with his outfit. After I bagged my mule deer, I helped Doug by tracking deer shot by other hunters. Mr. King offered me a job for the following year. For the next four years, I guided for deer and elk during the fall on the King's Ranch near Grand Junction, Colorado, returning home to further my college education each spring. I lived in a log cabin for four months of the year. The cabin had no electricity, no running water, nor any of the comforts of home, and I loved it! I cooked my own meals each day on a woodstove and made a shower out of a fifty-five-gallon drum, that is, when I got tired of bathing from a bucket. The only people I saw were the hunters Mr. King would bring for me to guide. Most of my time was spent getting the camp ready for hunters and scouting for deer and elk. My only transportation was a horse, whom I talked to pretty regularly, as I rode him scouting and checking on the cattle, sheep, and fences. On one occasion, I took the money I had made from guiding and left Colorado to go on a pack trip for elk in the Bitterroot Mountains of Idaho. For a young man, I was living a dream!

I finally finished college in 1982. Although I made a lot of poor decisions in my life, I thank God for always being there! One of my favorite verses of scripture is: "Be strong and courageous, do not be afraid or in dread of them, for the LORD your God is the One who is going with you. He will not desert you or abandon you" (Deuteronomy 31:6 [New American Standard Bible]).

God never failed nor forsook me. If He had not been with me while I was safeguarding from evil the natural resources He blessed us with, I might not be here today. And you might not be reading this book.

Most of the names and places mentioned in the book have been changed, to protect the guilty, so to speak. I have thoroughly enjoyed putting pen to paper through the writing of this book. I hope that people reading this book will either choose to do right with our natural resources or pursue a career conserving them. And I hope that everyone will better understand and respect God, who has allowed us to be the stewards of all of these wonderful resources He has given us.

THE POACHER'S NIGHTMARE

CHAPTER 1

A GAME WARDEN IN THE MAKING

It was 1976. I was sixteen and had been trapping since I was eight years old. The area called Plumber's Slough had been one of my favorite sites as it was full of beaver, coons, otter, and mink. Plumber's Slough was a large drainage that ran into Pelahatchie Creek, where it opened into the Ross Barnett Reservoir in Fannin, Mississippi.

I knew the local game wardens well, as I talked with them regularly. The wardens generally drank coffee at a little bait shop located near Pelahatchie Creek. I could only imagine having a job like theirs. They picked at me when I came through, warning that they were going to "catch me," as several of the locals said I was an "outlaw" due to the number of deer and turkey I killed. I did not headlight, but I couldn't count very well (limits!), nor did I understand what "POSTED" meant, especially if there was an old gobbler singing across the fence.

It was mid-December, around 5:30 a.m., as I parked my vehicle on the side of Spillway Road near the Ross Barnett Reservoir. I started dismantling the double-barreled 20-gauge shotgun that I frequently used to kill a few ducks while checking traps. The area I was trapping had recently been closed to hunting due to homes being built in the area. Oh, but those mallards kept rafting up in the coves, and the temptation was just too much! I would creep up on the unsuspecting mallards and gadwall, giving them both barrels of heavy load #6 shot. Ducks would start flopping!

While dismantling the little 20-gauge, I heard something out of the ordinary in the predawn stillness; it sounded like footsteps as the gravel crunched. Thinking quickly, I shoved the gun under the seat of the old International Scout that I drove at the time, closed the door, and started getting my trapping gear, when a light popped on and the deep voice of a game warden asked, "What are you doing with that gun?" I responded, "I was hiding it so no one would steal it." Warden Billy Moody stated, "I've been hearing you shoot back in here; I know you've been shooting ducks and I'm going to catch you." I denied that I had been shooting any ducks. The warden checked my gear and license and again warned, "I'm gonna catch you!" That was a close one!

Warden Moody never caught me, although I continued to take the double-barrel, slip into the swamp, and fire both barrels simultaneously into the rafted mallards. Not getting greedy by shooting too much, I evaded the wardens. I would pick up my ducks, hide them and the gun, and then check my traps coming out to the truck with only my catch of fur. Although I got checked several times, I never got caught shooting ducks.

It was my freshman year at the University of Southern Mississippi. I had not purchased a trapping license for the current trapping season. I called Warden Moody and asked if he would meet me at the local bait shop the following morning so I could purchase my license and start setting traps. I was going home for several weeks for the Christmas holidays and was anxious to start trapping. Warden Moody told me it would be midmorning before he would be able to meet me.

I told him where I was planning to start setting traps and asked if I could go ahead and start setting. Warden Moody agreed and told me he would blow his horn when he arrived at my truck with the license.

I pulled up to the Plumber's Slough bridge at daylight the following morning. It was one of those perfect December days, about forty-two degrees, blue skies, and a good forecast for the next few days. All that a trapper could ask for! A pack basket full of #11 long springs for mink and coon and a few #4s for beaver. I was excited because fur prices were high!

I had made several sets and, with nothing but the sounds of a few wood ducks whistling and the occasional squirrel barking, everything was quiet. Almost too quiet! As I finished making a mink set under some roots along the ditch bank, I paused. Scanning the hardwoods that surrounded me, I noticed an odd shape on the side of a large beech tree. As I continued to focus on the shape, it moved! It was the bill of a cap, and the profile of someone's face took shape. I spoke, asking the person to come out, wondering who they were and why they were watching me.

The man spoke, identifying himself as a game warden as he approached me. I recognized him as the supervisor of the warden I was supposed to meet, Warden Moody. He said sternly, "Let me see your license." I told him the situation and that Warden Moody was supposed to be bringing my license. Warden Edwards laughed and said, "Follow me to the truck, you're going to get a ticket,

The fur boom of the late 1970s led to my introduction to wildlife and their habits and habitats.

boy, for trapping without a license. I got you this time." I tried to explain, but I did not change the warden's mind. I stood at his truck while he wrote my ticket and picked at me about how they had been after me.

I took the ticket, got in my vehicle, and drove to the bait shop up the road where Warden Moody, whom I was supposed to meet, was drinking coffee with a couple of deputies and another warden I'd met before. I was trying to explain the situation to Warden Moody as Warden Edwards walked in, speaking out sarcastically as he poured his coffee, "Buy your license and get on boy!" Warden Moody wouldn't even look at me, as he knew what was going on and it was his boss who was calling the shots. It was very evident that each of the wardens knew what was going on. They all had known me for years, because they all drank coffee at my grandfather's bait shop about ten miles down the road. I bought my license and with a disgusted look left the store to get back to setting my traps.

On court day, I pled not guilty; the game warden was not expecting me to show up and ask for a trial. It was my first time in a courtroom, and I was scared to death! I represented myself before Judge Jones in the county court. The prosecutor got through with Warden Edwards's testimony of how he caught me setting traps and how I was required by law to have a license when I set traps. Warden Moody was there, and when I got my chance to speak, I asked

I started trapping when I was eight years old.

I always enjoyed fishing with my father—those were special times.

Trapping led to other benefits such as hunting and learning about wildlife (nice buck on the trapline).

I enjoyed trapping during Christmas holidays while in college.

A dependable means of travel was important on the trapline.

the judge if I could ask Warden Moody some questions. I can still remember the prosecutor leaning over, asking Warden Edwards, "What is he doing?"

Warden Moody took the stand, and I asked him, "Were you supposed to come to where I was setting traps that morning to sell me a trapping license, as per our phone call the night before?" "Yes," he said. I asked, "Did we discuss me going ahead and setting traps? Also, that you would blow your horn when you got to my truck and I would come out to buy my license?" "Yes, and yes," he said, looking down. The judge's face was getting red!

Asking me to stop, Judge Jones said, "Warden Edwards, approach the bench." I didn't know what was happening. The judge quietly asked, "Is this true what this boy is saying?" Warden Edwards, looking down, said, "The law says he is required to have a license whenever he is setting traps." It was evident that Judge Jones was upset. He told Warden Moody that he'd heard enough and was dismissing the charges against me, and he rapped his gavel hard on the bench! After the trial was over, the judge had some strong words for the warden who had issued the citation; a courtroom full of people whispered and giggled at the warden as the judge made his opinions known.

I had won that round, but I knew they would be after me for sure now. It was evident by the look the two wardens gave me as they exited the courthouse. They tried, but never had any luck.

That day in court, I would never have believed that the next time I would be before Judge Jones, I would be wearing a game warden's uniform. What a life, unknown to me then what roads I would travel as God opened the doors. God is good!

CHAPTER 2

THE JOB OF A LIFETIME

After graduating from college, I had an opportunity to work for the Mississippi Department of Wildlife, Fisheries, and Parks (MDWFP) as a fisheries technician. Mr. Tom, who was employed by the department's fisheries division, had told my father about the position. The fisheries technician job was not exactly what I wanted, but Mr. Tom told me that if I could get my foot in the door, I could transfer to law enforcement when a job became vacant.

I had never been to a formal job interview before and was very nervous. When I entered the room, there were five men in uniforms sitting in a semicircle with one empty chair facing them. I sat down and, after the introductions, Mr. Herring started the questions. They asked all types of questions involving fish biology that I had no idea of how to answer. However, I had spent a lot of time fishing on the Pearl River and the Ross Barnett Reservoir and was very familiar with those bodies of water and operating boats. The last question that was asked came from Mr. Bratford. I wasn't sure about it. Mr. Bratford asked, "What size boots do you wear?" I thought just a minute and responded, "Whatever size you got." From the response of the men at the interview, I must have answered it correctly. They all laughed and told me I was excused and to send in the next man from the waiting area on my way out. Undoubtedly, they were either impressed with something, or the other guys that put in for the position were worse than I was. I received a call a couple of days later verifying that I had gotten the job and when and where to report.

I started work as a fisheries technician in July 1983 at the Turcotte Fisheries Research Lab near the Ross Barnett Reservoir on the Pearl River. My first supervisor was a fisheries biologist named Willie. Willie oversaw collecting fisheries data on state lakes, reservoirs, and streams. My job consisted of shocking (electrofishing) fish, setting nets, and spraying aquatic vegetation. I got to do what I thought was fun—collecting data for the biologists. Who would have thought it; the stuff I used to slip around to do for fun, I now was getting paid to do! Kind of comical.

On one occasion, I was asked by a biologist doing a study on hybrid striped bass to help set nets on the Ross Barnett Reservoir. The biologist had no knowledge of the reservoir; he knew nothing about how to fish on the lake or where the old river runs were located. I, being the "grunt," didn't say anything, just did what I was told.

Tim, the biologist, was setting 1.5-inch monofilament webbing, and it just filled up with little catfish. We spent hours trying to get all those little blue cats out of the nets, with lots of sore hands from the needle-sharp fins afterward. We caught no hybrids! The biologist in charge of the hybrid bass program was from Ohio, and I was wondering, who taught this Yankee to set nets? I suggested to him to use 2.5- to 3-inch webbing and to try setting perpendicular to the main dam. After several more sets with the small webbing and some long days pulling fish, the biologist was willing to try anything. He let me take some 3-inch webbing and make a few sets. Tim did not even go. The following day, we loaded up with hybrids! The biologist was pleased; he had his fish and was able to place telemetry units in the fish for tracking them in the reservoir. He did ask how I knew where to set nets. I told him, "Just a lucky guess." Ha!

They did what at that time were called fish population studies. A crew of biologists and technicians would set a large net that, from the shoreline and corner to corner, would block off one acre of water. We then placed a chemical called rotenone in the water. When the fish swam through the chemical, it would get on their gills, not allowing the fish to get oxygen; therefore, they would die and rise to the water's surface. That's when the fun began! There would be three or four boats dipping fish—all the fish! If it was big enough to see, it got dipped! We separated each species, then measured by length and weighed them. That was the first day; the second day was not too enjoyable. Upon arrival, the smell from dead fish would be awful, and the same procedure would be repeated as on day one. Every fish from darters to the largest buffalo or carp was measured and weighed. The second day's pickup was always nasty. I never knew there were so many species of freshwater fish. My time with the fisheries division taught me many things that would help to further my career with the MDWFP.

Transfer to the Game Division: Alligator Position

While I was still employed as a fisheries technician, a wildlife biologist named Jim Lipe was hired and stationed at Turcotte Lab. Jim was in charge of the

Pearl River Wildlife Management Area (PRWMA), several counties involved in the Deer Management Assistance Program (DMAP), and the furbearer and alligator programs. With my interest in trapping, Jim and I became very good friends. When Jim started catching nuisance alligators, I was really interested but didn't get too involved initially because Jim always had plenty of help.

One day at the lab, Jim was talking about a particular gator they couldn't catch. The gator was in a relatively small lake and had become very shy to lights and the sound of people and would just sink to the bottom. As Jim was complaining about the gator, I spoke up and said, "I can catch him." After a little bit of an argument, Jim said, "We'll just see tonight!" I said, "We don't have to wait 'til dark; I'm pretty sure I can catch him in the daylight." Egos were starting to swell as Jim said, "Let's go!" I got permission from my supervisor and went and made a pole with a treble hook and heavy cord taped to the end. Jim did not have much faith but was willing to let me try.

When we arrived at the lake, the gator was visible on the other side of it. Jim and I put a small boat in the water and started toward the gator. The gator went under; Jim made a couple of remarks, and I continued to paddle toward where the gator was last seen. I stood up in the boat and, pointing at the bubbles coming up in the muddy water, whispered, "There he is." Jim was frowning like I was crazy. I eased my pole over the side of the boat to the bottom and slowly inched the pole along. I stopped, looked at Jim with a grin, and quietly said, "There he is." With a quick snatch on the pole, bubbles took off away from the boat as the rope taped to the pole was ripped away by the large gator, with a treble hook now wedged tightly into his hide. I said, "We got him!"

The fight was on for a while until the gator started to wear down. I slowly eased the rope toward the surface. The gator was hooked right behind the front left leg. Jim took the snare pole and slowly slipped a $3/32''$ cable snare over the unknowing gator's tail, as his head was still submerged under the thick vegetation. With a good jerk on the snare pole, he was secured.

We paddled the little boat back and pulled the nine-foot beast ashore. I held the rope tight while Jim secured the business end (his mouth) with electrical tape! We tied him head to tail and placed him in the back of the truck.

On the way back to the lab, Jim asked, "Where did you learn that trick?" I kind of laughed, not telling him much other than that I had fooled with a few gators growing up. Jim, having been raised a hunter and a fisherman, didn't want to ask too much. He might learn things he did not want to know! We laughed while heading back to the PRWMA to release the gator.

Jim and I became closer friends with every gator we caught. Due to the number of nuisance gator complaints, the agency decided to establish a position dedicated to handling them. It wasn't hard to figure out who should get

Jim Lipe and I with one of the first nuisance alligators we caught together. (Photo courtesy of the MDWFP.)

that job! Even better, I had gone from getting to set nets and shocking fish to catching gators and getting paid for it! God is good!

During that time, I was sent to the Mississippi Law Enforcement Training Academy and was now a law enforcement officer as well. Jim and I set up and taught a class together for in-service and new game wardens on catching and handling nuisance gators and other wildlife.

We had caught hundreds of gators by this time and were going to Louisiana to learn more about their agent trapper program. This program allowed for non-state-employed persons to be contracted by the state to answer complaints and remove nuisance alligators. The gator population across Louisiana had reached the point that no more needed to be relocated. The agent trappers were not paid a salary but could kill and skin the nuisance gators and sell the meat and hide for their pay. With the high prices being paid for gator hides, there were plenty of applicants. The program had its problems but did help, as the local game wardens did not have to answer all the complaints. We spent many hours catching alligators as well as being sent all over Louisiana to help or teach someone how to catch nuisance wildlife before returning to Mississippi.

Relocating nuisance alligators was a regular part of the job.

One gator complaint Jim received involved a man in the Mississippi Delta region of the state who believed that an alligator was eating his calves. Jim told me, and we both had a good laugh, not believing the man. Jim and I loaded up and headed to the flatlands. A neighboring landowner, along with several local game wardens, met us at the site of the complaint. The owner of the property was a very humble man; he did not claim that the gator was twenty feet long, as did some of the people who complained. He just said he had seen it on the bank of an old oxbow lake that came into his pasture and that he was missing several calves.

After sunset, Jim and I launched a small boat and got out our spotlight. We soon spotted the gator and headed to the "red glow" from the light reflecting from the gator's eyes. Everything worked smoothly as we eased up to the gator, blinded by the light, and placed a snare on the unsuspecting beast. The fight was on as we pulled him to where the landowners and others were waiting on shore. After Jim and I finished securing the gator, the landowner said, "I sure thought he was bigger than that." The gator only measured nine feet, two inches. Jim told the landowner that it was unlikely that alligator was eating calves.

We decided we would make another swing up on the lake and see if we could locate another alligator, mainly to satisfy the landowner. After getting a short distance into the trees, we spotted a "red glow," and, due to the angle the gator was facing, he didn't appear to be very large. Jim asked me to "call" (make a grunting sound like a young gator in distress) to him and see if he would turn toward us, as we were slowly getting close enough to snare. As the gator slowly turned, both Jim and I were shocked at the size of the monster, and we were only in a ten-foot aluminum boat! It was obvious that this gator was longer than our boat!

Jim eased the snare over the monster's head and gave a good, secure pull to tighten the snare. That gator didn't even go under! He rolled a couple of times and just lay there looking at us, as if he were contemplating what he was going to do next. Thankfully, we had plenty of rope. We just slowly backed out toward the bank, giving slack to the gator. After reaching the bank, we (Jim, myself, game wardens, and anyone else available) started to pull on the rope. Then the gator started to fight, and he was about to pull everyone in the water.

We decided to tie the rope to a truck belonging to one of the game wardens and slowly pull the gator out. Thankfully, there were no trees or snags in the way. He was pulling the truck side to side as he started to roll in the open water. What a show! As he was pulled about half out of the water, another snare was placed over his head to make sure we didn't lose this monster. As Jim got straddle of the gator and I lifted his head to secure his mouth, Jim's feet were barely touching the ground on each side. When secured, that beast measured thirteen feet, three inches, and weighed over 850 pounds. What a gator! Jim told the landowner he believed that gator could definitely have eaten calves. We released him into the Mississippi River. That was the largest gator Jim and I ever caught, or anyone else at that time in Mississippi.

With all the alligators that Jim and I had caught, from hatchlings to the thirteen-plus-foot, 850-pound giant, we had some close calls but were fortunate not to be severely injured. As with anything people do over and over again, I got complacent. I suppose I started to think I was invincible.

I received a call from the Rankin County Sheriff's Department concerning a nine-foot gator in someone's flowerbed near the Ross Barnett Reservoir. I headed to the call and met a game warden at the location. The alligator had attracted quite a bit of attention. There were deputy sheriffs, the reservoir patrol, and neighbors at the scene. They also told me that the local television news station was on its way. I tried to pull the gator out by its tail, but due to its size and the way it was dug into the shrubs and other vegetation, I was not successful. Needless to say, I wasn't getting any offers for help.

A rookie, Warden Neil, was there to help. I told the warden to place a towel I had fixed to a board over the gator's eyes. After the warden had the eyes covered, I got straddle of the gator and started easing up its length. With the way I was positioned, if the gator decided to get aggressive, I could stay clear of the business end! I had placed a rubber strap on my left shoulder that I would use to secure the mouth once I had the gator under control.

Everything was going well as I started slowly reaching for the jaws of the seemingly lifeless creature. As I went to grab for the gator's mouth, Neil accidentally moved the towel, exposing its eyes. The same time I grabbed for the jaws, the gator opened its mouth, so I grabbed only the upper jaw. A quick "snap!" and both of my hands were crushed between the jaws of the gator, and the once seemingly lifeless creature was very much alive!

The gator started trying to roll with both of my hands between its viselike jaws. Alligators have sharp but round teeth (puncture and crush), and after they clamp, they use their body weight to twist and tear off whatever their prey may be. As the gator started to roll, I knew that if I did not get my hands from his mouth, he would tear them off.

Fortunately, the gator didn't weigh more than I was able to handle, at least for a minute or two. As the struggle continued, the gator snapped its jaws and my right hand became free, but the left was still full of gator teeth and in its jaws. I grabbed with my right hand under the gator's lower jaw and was able to pull its head back. This motion causes the animal to become temporarily lethargic, as the blood rushes to the brain, which is very much like putting a toad on its back.

As I sat on the gator's back with my left hand still in its mouth, I was able to slide the strap down my left arm and over its mouth. Now the only problem was, my left hand was stuck in the gator's mouth! As some of the other officers came to assist once its mouth was secure, I looked over into the left side of the gator's mouth, not sure what I would find. Fortunately, when he snapped the second time, my left hand made it most of the way out of the gator's mouth!

16   The Job of a Lifetime

Even after retirement, I still worked to relocate nuisance alligators.

When the gator clamped the second time, it bit through most of the tissue but had a tooth hung longways in my ring finger. With a little pulling, I was able to rip my left hand from the gator's mouth. There weren't many people trying to help, other than the deputies drawing their guns. Easy to find out who your friends are in these situations!

I wrapped my hands with a clean cloth to cover as much of the blood as possible. Adding humor to the situation, some people thought the alligator was the injured one. Undoubtedly, because of the way the gator was behind the shrubbery, they didn't realize that my hands had been in the beast's mouth!

After the gator was loaded into my truck, I asked the warden to drive me to the emergency room of River Oaks Hospital. I was a frequent visitor to be stitched up and knew most of the staff personally. After arriving at the ER and explaining the circumstances, the staff left me bleeding to go and admire the alligator! After X-rays were taken, the young ER doctor started cleaning the punctures and ripped flesh with what appeared to be betadine; he said that was the first gator wound he'd ever treated. I emphasized the massive amounts of bacteria inside gators' mouths. It was bad stuff . . . nasty! The doctor scrubbed and used long swabs saturated with betadine to clean into and through the wounds. After a thorough cleaning and several shots, he stitched up the holes and sent me on my way.

Once back in my vehicle, I had to go and release the gator. On my radio, I got word that the news media was going to be at the boat landing to do an interview concerning the "gator attack!" Oh, how quickly things got blown out of proportion. I spoke with a reporter, but due to the fact there were no limbs or fingers missing, it wasn't much of a story. After all, planes that land safely don't make the news! Also, I told them that the gator did not attack me; I just cut my hands while catching it. Not quite the story they were looking for, huh?

I did feel a bit odd while talking to the reporter. I thought it must have been from the antibiotics or something they gave me at the hospital. I went home, and a long night of high fever and a severe illness followed. I decided the following morning to go to the local fire department and get one the emergency medical technicians to check me out. After giving me a quick once-over and smelling my hand—that's right, smelling my hand—they told me to get back to the ER ASAP!

They offered a ride in the ambulance, but I refused because my dad was with me, so we headed that way. There were nurses waiting at the door when we arrived. They quickly decided to call in a specialist to deal with the infection that had started in my hands and was spreading through my body. The last thing I remembered as they rolled me away to surgery was the doctor telling

Kennie putting out a net for a rotenone survey. Photo by James L. Cummins.

my parents that he would try to save my left hand, but it was bad, and that a lot of tissue would have to be removed as it was starting to rot.

 I recovered from that encounter, but it was not the last. The doctors at the ER at least learned how to treat a gator bite. The other bites weren't quite as bad but did require a few stitches. I kept all my fingers. God protects even the foolish sometimes!

CHAPTER 3

LAW ENFORCEMENT: NEVER A DULL DAY!

It was 1989 and a position opened, finally, in Rankin County for a conservation officer, and I got to become a full-time game warden. I was very proud of my position, feeling like John Wayne walking around in that uniform. I loved my job!

The previous positions and experience with the fisheries and game divisions were educational, and the biological knowledge I received was very useful in my career. Being close to a large body of water and the City of Jackson meant no downtime. A lot of wardens across the state did not have lakes, rivers, or large bodies of water nearby and would get bored when the hunting seasons closed, unless they were sent to help us.

Boating presented all kinds of challenges. Most people thought that a game warden just checked fishing licenses; not quite. Wardens working areas like the Ross Barnett Reservoir or any of the other large water bodies were always involved in much more. It could get exciting when you least expected it.

In one specific encounter, Warden Neil and I approached a houseboat that had several ski boats tied to it. We were going to do a routine safety check of boat registrations, personal floatation devices, and the like. As we approached the vessel, we noticed people frantically running and jumping into the ski boats and speeding away. By the time Neil was able to get on the houseboat, all but the person who owned the boat were gone. In trying to assess the situation and questioning the captain of the vessel, we noticed a white, powdery substance on the main table that was later proven to be cocaine. Just another day on the lake!

Narcotics, boat wrecks, drownings, missing persons, and fights made for some long days and nights; reports of shots fired were common enough. Intoxicated individuals and domestic disputes meant problems. Some of it was exciting; some of it was very depressing.

On one occasion I got a call concerning a possible drowning that turned into much more. The MOB (man overboard) call came through the reservoir patrol. It was midsummer during the middle of the week. There was very little boat traffic that day. As I drove up to the landing, with my patrol boat in tow, there were numerous law enforcement officers present. Reservoir patrol and Rankin County deputies were at the landing getting information from the operator of the boat who had made the call.

As I got out of my truck and approached, the officers gathered around the man. I recognized the subject. We had met a few weeks earlier, when I had stopped him and some other subjects on the river. The subject had been very intoxicated and was arrested.

As I was talking with the deputy who had the relevant information, the subject was loading his boat. I tried to tell the officer in charge that something might be up. The subject's demeanor was not that of someone who had just had a friend fall overboard. He was leaving! His friend has just drowned and he's leaving, I thought. Strange.

The subject had taken one of the officers out on the water to mark where he said his friend had fallen in. As I was launching my boat, he looked at me with a grin on his face and said, "Good fishing!" Again, I told the older deputy that they might want to hold the subject for further questioning. He told me that they had no reason and that they needed to start search and rescue operations. The subject drove away and waved at me, still with a grin on his face, not to be seen again. I was very frustrated and unsure of what was actually taking place. The officer in charge had only a first name for the MOB.

As usual, the local news stations had picked up the possible drowning and search that was about to take place on their scanners. Here they come! Local volunteer groups, here they come! Not to say that volunteers weren't a great help on occasion, but sometimes they got in the way. When you had local media present, there was always jostling as to who was in charge, or appeared to be, among agencies such as the Sheriff's Department, reservoir patrol, and game and fish agencies.

By this time in my career, I had worked numerous drownings, and when the missing person was out on the open water, seldom did you find the body until it floated up. Finding a body in water could sometimes take up to three days, depending on water temperature. With thirty-three thousand acres of water in the Ross Barnett Reservoir, searching for the body could be a great task, even when it surfaced.

The subject had carried the officer to the location where the man had supposedly fallen out of the boat, but by the time the search started it was pretty clear that we would have to wait for the body to float. What I did not know was that the family of the man they were searching for had been located and were waiting at the landing. The search team continued its work late into the night. The news reporters and the family at the landing made it hard to just quit, even though most of us knew it was going to be several days.

The following day we again found nothing and, with the novelty of the search wearing off, most of the volunteers and media left. This was normal for those types of searches... just the "old game wardens" stuck around. Warden Wegner and I had worked numerous drownings together and, on the third morning, we knew it was getting close to time for the body to float.

There was a reporter who wanted to ride with us. As reporters tend to do, she asked questions. Warden Wegner and I, along with the reporter, boarded our boat and headed across the lake. The lake was like glass, with just a small roll. The reporter was sitting on the middle seat next to me, but facing back toward Warden Wegner, who was operating the boat.

As we were crossing the lake at a pretty good speed, I spotted something breaking the water and directed Wegner in that direction. Wegner did not see the man's head and was still going pretty fast as I reached and grabbed the body, and I held on until he could get the boat stopped. The missing person was a big man, and it was all I could do to hold him.

As the boat came to a stop, I was able to pull the man's head over the edge of the boat, which made him easier to hold. The man's eyes were staring at us, with his swollen tongue protruding from his mouth. It was admittedly a nasty sight, let alone the smell, as we attempted to lift him from the water. The reporter undoubtedly had never seen a dead person before, outside of a funeral. She freaked out! Another patrol boat had to come and get the reporter before we could put the body in the boat and into a body bag.

The body of the man retrieved from the water was completely nude. His family said that he had been living on the streets and that they had never heard of the fellow who had taken him boating. Despite the questionable circumstances, the coroner ruled the cause of death to be drowning. The family tried to have the matter looked into further, but to no avail. The case was closed. The man who had been operating the boat was never seen again. We worked many drownings that were very suspicious, with the only witness being a surviving companion. Regarding the statement, "They just fell in and didn't come up," I always wanted to tell them, God knows what happened!

Boat-Car Wreck?

On one call, I received information from the dispatcher that a boat had hit a car. I asked the dispatcher to repeat and give the location. Dispatch confirmed, on north side of the causeway that crossed Pelican Bay. Upon arriving on the scene, I was astonished, as I saw a ski boat in the middle of the road with the bow broken up and a small sports car with a big dent in the passenger door. A reservoir patrol officer was approaching from the south side, and there were quite a few witnesses.

After speaking with the officer, we started questioning the driver of the car and some of the bystanders, as the boat operator was not to be seen. Some of the witnesses said that a man and woman who had been in the boat got into a vehicle and left the scene. After we looked through the boat, it was evident by the many empty beer cans that the operator may have been intoxicated.

This was a first for me; the boat had climbed up at least fifty feet of rip-rap (rocks), cleared the metal railing, and hit a moving car in broad daylight. As the name of the owner of the boat was coming back from dispatch after running the boat identification number, one of the bystanders said, "There he is." They pointed to a man walking onto the scene followed by a lady carrying a small baby. I began questioning the man, asking if anyone was hurt. The man was very reluctant to speak.

I asked the lady if she was okay. Something wasn't right, and, with the man's head bowed down, the lady spoke up: "Tell him, tell him everything!" Then, looking at me, she said, "I want a copy of the report when you're finished!," giving her name and phone number. I asked, "Ma'am, were you injured?" She responded, "I was not in the boat!" Uh oh! Things were coming together, as the man apparently had been trying to get the "other woman" off the scene before his wife arrived. The man operating the boat was apparently intoxicated and refused to give up the name of his female passenger. After placing him in handcuffs and sending him to the hotel (i.e., jail), he never did give up his female acquaintance. Hope it was worth it for him, as it appeared he was going to lose a lot more than a girlfriend.

Graveyard Shift!

After receiving complaints of shots being fired after dark near some soybean fields in southern Rankin County, I decided to set up behind an old church where I could see the fields. The long nights of sitting in the darkness waiting on someone to turn on a light or to hear a shot could sometimes get one's mind to wandering. The sounds in the darkness could be a little spooky, especially when set up between an old church and a cemetery! The hoot of a barred owl, howling coyotes in the distance, and a night so dark you could not see the ground tended to put one on edge.

I parked under a large pin oak, the constant clank of acorns hitting the roof of the truck keeping me alert as I stared across the soybean fields into the darkness. As I was waiting for something to happen, the clanking of acorns seemed a little odd, more like something bumping the truck. I looked into the side mirror only to see nothing, but the sound continued as if in the back of the truck!

As my senses were getting on edge, I slowly turned and looked over my right shoulder toward the bed of the truck; my eyes focused on another set of eyes only inches away! Before I could think, my truck was cranked, and I was slinging gravel up the county road! I knew what I had seen, but my nerves couldn't take any more and I reacted. A big house cat jumped or flew from the truck somewhere as I fled the scene. So much for the fearless game warden!

A few nights later found me sitting at the graveyard again. Not long after setting up, I heard the unmistakable crack of a .22 caliber rifle. I eased out of my truck and crossed the graveyard to the edge of the field, where I could see two lights working. Several shots later, I positioned myself along the edge of the field next to a big oak tree.

The subjects cut their lights off, and I saw their silhouettes crossing the field in my direction. Due to a low spot in the field, I could no longer see them but expected that they would cut across the field back toward the end where some houses were located. It seemed like forever as I squatted next to the tree, staring into the darkness trying to find them.

Just on the other side of the tree, I heard a limb snap. I slowly stood and peeked around the tree. I was face to face with a young fella, and I'm not sure who hollered first—me or him! Where the other guy went, I have no idea, but the chase was on, and I had never had someone outrun me! Yet!

As I was gaining on him in the darkness, I didn't see the six-foot ditch that he undoubtedly knew was there. I disappeared into the ditch, burying my head into the muddy bank on the far side (thought I'd broken my neck)! Needless to say, I don't know where he went. I can say, however, that I never got any more calls about headlighting in that field!

Big Black Cat

On another headlighting detail, I sat in the truck with my supervisor on another of those black nights. The only light was the flickering of the radio, as officers in distant areas made conversation. It was a very warm night for December; we both had the truck doors open as we surveilled a small wheat field where we had received complaints of poachers shooting deer after dark.

Simon, my supervisor, complained about the hip he'd recently had surgery on, as he kept moving around trying to find comfort. As he tried to straighten his leg out, he would stick it under the console below the radio. In doing so, he would bump me, and I kept picking at Simon about rubbing my leg.

In the distance, a cat was meowing and seemed to be getting closer. Simon and I joked about the cat, saying it must be an old tomcat looking for a girlfriend. The yowling continued in the distance throughout the night.

The night had been slow, with only an occasional vehicle passing the wheat field and none even slowing to look for deer. As Simon and I were about out of war stories, I felt what I thought was Simon's foot rubbing my leg. As I brought the rubbing to Simon's attention, he said, "What are you talking about, I'm not rubbing your leg!"

Just then, the claws from the wandering tomcat buried deep into my calf, and, before I could holler, a big black Persian cat was in my lap! Both Simon and I yelled as the tomcat then jumped over into Simon's lap and started purring and rubbing against him! We both laughed and thanked God we had heard the cat before the incident took place. We agreed that, if we could have reached our guns, someone would've found us both dead and wondered why we'd shot each other.

"Unusual Calls" (Weird Alligator?)

One day I received a call from the main office about an alligator in a ditch near a subdivision. It wasn't out of the norm to receive a call during the summer concerning alligators . . . just another day at the office! I took the address from dispatch and headed to the origin of the call.

As I pulled up to the complainant's residence, he came out to give me the location of the gator and his analysis of the situation. It was not uncommon for the person making a call to be quick to tell me what needed to be done! Mr. Jones said, angrily, "That gator is over there in the ditch near the box culvert. I watch him every day, but some kids were trying to kill him today! I ran them off and called your office." I said, "I'll move him." We walked over to the ditch, which was almost dried up, except for a large pool of muddy water between the walking trail and the road.

I had a little choke stick to subdue the gator and entered the water, poking around on the bottom to locate him, thinking he had just sunk to the bottom. After wading around with no luck, I noticed a trail going into a hole on one side of the box culvert. It appeared that something had been going in and out of there regularly. I went to my truck and got a flashlight to look into the hole.

Mr. Jones was watching as I stepped back into the ditch, wading up to the box culvert to see if I could locate the little alligator, as it's not uncommon for them to go into holes during the heat of the day, trying to get cool. I started looking up into the hole with my light. I could see a tail and a back leg, but there were no ridges on the tail. I looked up at Mr. Jones, asking, "Are you sure that's an alligator?" He quickly responded, "Son, I know what an alligator looks like!"

Still questioning what I was seeing, I thought, "Maybe it's just the darkness playing tricks on my eyes." I went back to my truck and got a shovel to dig the hole out big enough to pull the little gator out. After returning to the ditch and digging a little, I peeked back into the hole with my light. The culprit had moved a little further in, but I could reach his tail.

I handed Mr. Jones my shovel and told him, "Step back, I'm going to grab his tail and pull him out, planning to throw him up on the bank." I reached into the hole and, as soon as I felt his tail, quickly grabbed him and snatched him out of the hole and in the same motion threw him up on the bank. The creature (not an alligator) took off running toward the woods. I was in hot pursuit and dove on him, grabbing him behind the head with both hands!

Mr. Jones, breathing heavily, asked, "What the heck is that?" Rolling over on my butt, with a four-foot-long lizard in my lap still flopping around, I finally got his back legs and tail under my arm to get him completely subdued. I said, "I think he's a monitor lizard. I've only seen them on TV."

I carried the lizard back to my truck, where I was able to get on the radio and tell the dispatcher to send a herpetologist from the museum. "I need someone who can take this creature I've just caught and identify it. I think it's a monitor lizard." The dispatcher said, "A what? I'll get someone headed that way!"

I sat in my truck holding the creature, awaiting someone to take it. As the big lizard was somewhat disturbed, he regurgitated in my lap, covering me with fish and crawfish parts! That was definitely a nice aroma! The department herpetologist pulled up next to me and very excitedly said, "Wow, an aquatic monitor lizard! Where did you find him?" He took the lizard back to the Mississippi Museum of Natural Science and placed him in a holding facility.

After investigating further, we found out that someone had been admitted to one of the local emergency rooms after being bitten by an aquatic monitor lizard. We located the person, and he said that he had purchased the lizard as a pet, and, after it bit him, he released it in the reservoir about three months prior to my catching it. We scolded him pretty well about releasing nonnative wildlife into the area, but no charges were filed. We gave the lizard to the Jackson Zoo.

Betty (my wife) and Buddy McClain with a young kangaroo.

Kangaroo?

Being the local game warden, one receives all kinds of calls, from "I heard a black panther" to "I saw Bigfoot." Nothing surprised me anymore. I answered the phone one morning and the fella's first words were, "I don't drink!" I replied, "Do what?" He then responded, "I live in Reservoir West and, while I was drinking coffee this morning, a kangaroo hopped by my window!" I responded with a little chuckle, "A what?" He quickly came back, "I know what I saw!" I said, "I'll be over shortly."

I put on my uniform and headed that way. Not knowing what I was going to do with this situation, I called in to the dispatcher, saying, "I'm headed on a kangaroo call!" "Do what? Repeat," the dispatcher responded. I laughed and said, "Headed on a kangaroo call at Reservoir West subdivision." Dispatcher, "Okay!"

As I was turning into the subdivision, the statewide radio (Sheriff's Department) blurted out, "Someone just reported they hit a kangaroo in Reservoir West." Okay, maybe he wasn't nuts. I called dispatch on the radio and said, "Might need to call someone from the zoo, got a crippled kangaroo on the side of the road in Reservoir West!"

As I arrived at the scene, a sheriff's deputy pulled up. I'd never seen a kangaroo other than at the zoo and on TV. It seemed kind of small. As I was looking at it lying in the ditch, the deputy said, "I just saw another one cross the road." I looked down the road and, sure enough, there was another kangaroo standing in someone's front yard. I told the deputy to get in his car, circle the block, and stop any traffic from coming in from the other direction. We'd try not to spook it until someone from the zoo got there with a dart gun to tranquilize it.

We just kept an eye on it, trying to keep people from spooking it. Finally, a young lady from the zoo got there. She eased up to the wallaby, as she called it, and darted it. They are a relative of the kangaroo, just a smaller species. We were able to load it into a cage she had on her truck. The one that had been hit by a car had died. We later discovered that the wallabies had gotten out of a pen several miles away after a storm had blown a tree across the fence, allowing them to escape.

Don't Feed Wildlife!

On a special detail on the Mississippi Gulf Coast, the task force (a group of wardens who handled special details in all areas of the state) had been called on to try to apprehend some roe mullet fishermen who had shot at the local wardens on several occasions. Coastal marsh was something I wasn't used to, so I loved working in that part of the state. My partner that night was a seasoned officer with many years of experience, but he had never been in the coastal marsh and wetlands of Mississippi.

We were using unmarked equipment, and our boat was a fourteen-foot-long, five-foot-wide bottom aluminum craft with a forty horsepower Johnson outboard motor. It was my favorite boat, as it would fly! In the cover of darkness, we launched and slid into the night. I had marked all the canals and navigable areas on my GPS from an earlier trip with one of the local officers who had been shot at.

Joey, my partner for the night, was a little unsure about the detail, as he had never seen the area in the daytime. The night was going to be long, as we were prepared to stay until sunrise the following day, and the weather forecast didn't look too promising with a 60 percent chance of thunderstorms. As the forty-horsepower started winding up with me only looking down at the GPS, Joey started getting nervous, asking me to slow down, which only made me turn the throttle to wide open! Joey didn't trust the GPS, and the only things he could see were the channel markers as they flew past the boat. I slowed the boat, as I could tell Joey was getting a little rattled when he said, "Enough of this crap!" I just laughed and slowly eased in and out of the canals, stopping occasionally to listen for other boat traffic.

As we came to the edge of the marsh and what appeared to be lights near some homes, we pulled the boat under a big willow tree that hung into the canal and prepared for a long night on the river. You could see lightning across the Gulf of Mexico in the distance, and, as they rolled across the sky, the thunderheads in that direction were beautiful. It was if God were painting a different picture with each strike of lightning, and the pictures were steadily getting closer!

Joey asked what I thought we ought to do. I grinned and said, "Put on your rain gear!" With a look of disbelief, Joey grabbed his bag and started putting on his gear. I said while getting mine on, "Better hurry up. It will be here in a minute!" The thunderhead that had been so beautiful in the distance lost its grandeur when the wind, rain, and lightning were upon us.

We hunkered down on the floor of the boat. The waves tossed it around like a fishing cork. With the rain pouring down, I yelled to Joey, "Untie the boat!" He looked back like I was nuts. I said, "We have to float with the waves or we'll sink!" Joey took my advice, struggled to his feet, and untied the boat. Once the boat was free, I got it cranked, turned the bow into the incoming waves, and kept it facing into the wind.

As quickly as it came, the storm was gone. The thunderhead rumbled in the distance as it weakened farther inland. As we pulled back under the willow to take up our surveillance position, I said, "That was awesome!" Joey responded, "You're nuts!" I told Joey to just listen, as the frogs were getting so loud you could hardly hear anything above them. As Joey put his rain gear up, the clouds disappeared to reveal a sky full of stars.

I was still talking about the beauty of the night when Joey stated, "Look at that big coon, he's a big 'un." I looked at a big old coon coming from the direction of the houses made his way down the shoreline toward us. As he approached the boat, it was evident that someone had been feeding him; he showed no fear and would stand on his rear legs as if trying to see what we had that might be of interest. Joey threw him a cookie and laughed as he wobbled over and quickly consumed it. I warned Joey, but he kept throwing cookies as the coon got closer to the boat.

Once Joey quit throwing cookies to the fat bandit of the night, he decided he would come get some on his own. As he worked his way through the limbs of the willow tree toward the bow of the boat, I told Joey to take something and knock the coon out of the tree. Joey just laughed and tossed some chips as the overweight coon dropped out of the willow onto the deck. Joey was having a good time, or at least he was until he ran out of treats for the bandit. Then, I had a show as the unhappy coon, smelling more to be had, and Joey were at a standoff. The coon was standing and growling as if he were six feet tall and intending to seize the boat. I then smacked him out of the boat with the paddle.

We moved up river, thinking we were out of reach of the bandit. Hours passed with nothing seen concerning the job at hand. After we ate a meal of tuna and crackers, a slow but steady rain started back and appeared to be setting in. I sat on the floor of the boat with my back against the seat next to the motor. Joey was on the floor of the boat in front of the middle seat. The night had gotten quiet, as we had stopped talking and started dozing off, even with the rain dripping from the bills of our rain gear.

My eyes popped open as I heard what sounded like a can bumping the side of the boat, then the clanking of metal against metal. I sat motionless, with all my senses focused on the sounds. Before I could figure the sound out, something was bumping and slowly pulling the side of my rain hood. Trying not to move and frighten whatever it was, I felt the cold paws of the raccoon pulling at my beard. The raccoon was undoubtedly getting some of the tuna and crackers that had dropped into my beard earlier in the night!

Frozen, trying not to scare the coon and make a bad situation worse, I whispered, "Joey . . . Joey." Joey finally answered, but he didn't look back. "What?" he said. I said quietly, "Get up slow and get the paddle." Joey realized that something was wrong and slowly turned around, seeing the coon digging and licking at my beard. His first reaction was a slight snicker, as the coon was now on my shoulder looking back at Joey with a slow rumbling growl. Joey poked at the coon with the paddle, and, once his attention was on Joey, I slung the coon into the river.

Joey was laughing so hard, had there been any illegal activities going on in that county, our position would have been compromised. It was a long night to gain nothing but a little knowledge of "DON'T FEED WILDLIFE!"

I Can Only Imagine!

One afternoon in late October, I received a call from the sheriff's office about a possible missing hunter. As a game warden, it was not uncommon once hunting season opened to get calls of this nature. We (game wardens) always joked that if it was off the blacktop or on the water, call the game warden! We were the ones who would go into the swamps or wherever a person may have gone missing; not that some of the deputies wouldn't help, but if it involved the woods, they would always call us.

As I pulled up on Flemming Road, Warden Neil pulled in behind me. There were two deputy sheriff's cars and two other vehicles at the scene. One of the deputies was advising me of the situation when a fellow I recognized stepped up. I had once caught his son headlighting rabbits on Christmas Eve, and rather than taking him to jail, I called his father to come get him, wishing them a "Merry Christmas." Mr. Evans, whose father was now missing, came forward and called me by name, as he had not forgotten our contact from the year before, either.

Mr. Evans said, "My father went squirrel hunting this morning and when I got home from work, he wasn't there. I found his car here where he normally parks. Daddy is seventy-eight years old and I'm worried about him; I've been calling for him and he won't answer, I'm afraid he's lost!" It was dark by this time. The deputy had also been calling out over his public address unit, with no response. Warden Neil, one of the deputies, and I got our flashlights and entered the woods to search.

I said, "It's been dry, he's probably following the old logging road that runs through the hardwoods. I'll stay on the road and y'all each stay within sight of me and we'll work the road first." They agreed. We entered the woods, and I started following the dim trail of an old logging road through the hardwood bottom, with them working each side. We slowly worked our way deep into the darkness. The stillness was broken only by footsteps in the dry fall leaves, occasional radio traffic on one of our walkie talkies, or the hoot of a barred owl in the depth of the woods. I always loved being in the woods at night! There was just a peace that always came with it.

We hadn't gone more than a couple hundred yards, slowly sweeping our lights along the forest floor, checking every tree, when I noticed something next to a large white oak. The elder Mr. Evans was sitting at the bottom of the big hardwood tree with his shotgun across his lap as if he were asleep. I spoke out to the others involved in the search: "Over here!" As they were approaching, I checked for a pulse on his neck and he was cold to the touch. He looked as though he had just fallen asleep, with his head tilted a little forward. I told the deputy to go back, call the coroner, and get a body bag; also, if Mr. Evans's son wanted, he could follow him back.

While they were gone, I sat and thought, "What a way to go." He was sitting there doing something he loved, and the Lord called him home. I thought, "I hope when the Lord calls me home, it's something like this, sitting in a beautiful hardwood bottom with the beauty of fall, enjoying all that God has blessed us with!"

When Mr. Evans's son returned, he was visibly upset. It is never easy when a family member has to identify someone they love. I did tell him what I had been thinking, while waiting: "What a peaceful way to go home to the Lord." His only response was, "Daddy loved to come down here and squirrel hunt as long as I can remember. Thank you for finding him." All I could say was, "I'm sorry for your loss!"

It Was Crappie Time!

During late March, the crappie would really go to biting if the conditions were right, and those die-hard crappie anglers were very persistent, fishing every day. It was a busy time for game wardens, also, checking licenses and counting fish. Some anglers had a hard time counting when crappie began biting!

It was one of those spring days when you couldn't ask for anything better. Not a cloud in that beautiful blue sky, winds were calm, water was like glass, and the temperature was approximately seventy-eight degrees. I had been in a boat earlier that morning doing routine patrol to check licenses and limits and the like, had dropped my boat at home around eleven o'clock, and then went to check boat landings at the upper end of the reservoir.

As I drove across the reservoir on Highway 43, the "welfare hole," as it is called by local anglers, was covered with boats. I stopped and glassed them, seeing them land a few (they weren't wearing them out). I checked several landings, then went up to check some of the river landings. Several hours had passed before I made my way back down the Natchez Trace Parkway to Highway 43 and headed back across the reservoir.

I pulled over again to glass the "welfare hole." There were about half the number of boats that had been there earlier. Those left were the die-hard, all-day anglers! I did notice one fisherman who was away from the others and appeared to be tied to a stump. I made another loop, stopping at one of the local bait shops, and decided to make one more stop on Highway 43 before calling it a day. As I pulled over at the "welfare hole," I noticed that fisherman still tied to the stump and thought, "He must be catching them, he's been there for at least six hours."

I got my binoculars and started watching him. As I stared through my binoculars, he never moved. I got out where I could look across the hood of my truck. The more I focused on him, the more it appeared that the hand he was holding the pole with was open and the end of the pole was in the water. Something was not right!

I headed to the closest landing and asked a fisherman there to take me out on the reservoir so I could make sure that the fisherman in the boat was alright. As we approached his boat, it was evident that he was dead! He was still sitting in his boat with his pole in hand, facing east. He looked as though he had just drifted off to sleep. I guess he couldn't have had a better day of fishing when the Lord called him home!

CHAPTER 4

YOU'RE LATE! A DOVE CASE RESULTED IN A FRIENDSHIP

My daddy loved dove hunting and was an excellent wing shot. Growing up, we hunted doves throughout each season and bagged quite a few, although we weren't very good at counting sometimes. When I was about sixteen years old, Daddy was invited to a big dove hunt at a very prominent individual's place. At that time, you couldn't shoot doves until after 12:00 noon, and on some of the bigger hunts we went to they would have a big cookout before the hunt. It was a very social event, as it signaled the beginning of that year's hunting seasons. At this particular hunt, I remember distinctly that there were several politicians, bankers, and even game wardens at the cookout. Daddy asked our host, Mr. Patrick, about the game wardens. I'm not sure what precisely he asked, but I remember Mr. Patrick saying, "Y'all shoot all you want to, they won't bother you."

As we stood around where lunch was being served, in a large pecan grove near the prepared dove field, the power lines were sagging with doves. I thought to myself, "We're gonna kill some birds today!" After 12:00, Daddy, my cousin Butch, and I went to the field, and hundreds of doves were flying. I had never seen that many doves before.

By 3:00 p.m., my hunting vest was heavy with birds, as well as the bucket I had carried into the field. Daddy walked over and angrily said, "Get your stuff, we're leaving! You and Butch take all the doves, walk out in the woods, and I'll pick you up on the gravel road." He then counted out a limit of birds, putting them in his vest. I wondered why we were leaving but didn't ask. Before heading to the truck, he said, "This is not right; those guys are paid to enforce the law!" I was a bit confused, but I knew to do as I was told. I sure didn't want to leave! Daddy, Butch, and I all had well over the bag limit, and there were still several hours of good shooting left!

After picking Butch and me up, Daddy didn't say much other than, "Those guys are paid to enforce the law and they are sitting around drinking alcohol, and that's just not right." That was the last time Daddy or I ever shot over the limit of doves. It wasn't because we got caught, but I guess Daddy was so mad that the game wardens were just sitting there while we slaughtered doves and did nothing. At sixteen years old, that's a lesson I never forgot!

Many years later, after becoming a game warden, I worked the opening weekend with federal agents on some large, baited fields. It was the second weekend of the 1989 dove season and I just happened to be driving near the property of one of the Patrick family members. They always had several dove fields. I had been hearing shooting since daylight but could not locate its source.

The area was rural, consisting of primarily pastures and hayfields. I decided that if I was going to locate all that shooting, I would just have to walk and find it. I hid my marked truck in an old cutover, put on a camouflage jacket and a hunting vest, and grabbed my ticket book and binoculars. I went back to the blacktop, then headed up a gravel road that led to an old house trailer that appeared to be vacant. Getting off the gravel road, I walked along the edge of the cutover in an adjacent field.

As I passed the trailer, while focused on all the shooting, I heard a woman say, "You're late!" Surprised, I turned to see a group of women sitting and drinking coffee on a little porch attached to the trailer. I thought, "I'm busted." I spoke back, saying, "I couldn't find the field." I guess they didn't realize I wasn't carrying a shotgun. She responded, "Just follow the field road and it will take you there." I thanked them and continued along that way.

As I got to the crest of the hill, I could see at least eight vehicles parked together near the cutover. Only one vehicle was in the disked field they were hunting in. They were steadily shooting, and it was nearing 8:00 a.m. I knew I didn't have long. I got in the thick cutover and fought my way through the briars and poison ivy until reaching the vehicles. Crawling under one of the four-wheel-drive trucks, I could see just about every hunter in the field.

I started counting drops and, by 9:00 a.m., I knew at least two of the hunters had gone over the limit. They were wearing the doves out! The vehicle that was parked in the disked area started out of the field. My plan was to just let him go because I hadn't noticed him killing many birds. When the vehicle came through the fenced gap, he stopped at the vehicle I was hiding under and got out to relieve himself. While doing so, he spotted me under the truck. He asked, "What the heck are you doing under there?" I showed him my badge saying, "I'm a game warden." Hoping he wouldn't alert the other hunters, I asked him to show me his license and never got out from under the truck. He was very cooperative.

After checking his license, I asked him to leave the field. I never actually looked at the name on the license—it was Mr. Patrick. He was the owner of the property and the brother of the owner of the field I mentioned earlier where I'd hunted with my daddy. He responded, "Can I come back? I want to see this." A little confused, I said, "If you don't mind, head on out like you were doing." He did as I asked and drove on over the hill.

The shooting had started to slow down by 10:00 a.m., and I could see the hunters gathering their gear and starting to make their way back to the vehicles. I had gotten behind the farthest vehicle. As each hunter walked up, I identified myself, asking them to place their guns and gear next to the fence and show me their hunting license. At first, things were a little tense, to say the least, as several of the hunters were not too happy. I had twelve hunters' guns and gear next to the fence, with one individual still making his way toward the vehicles. He just couldn't stop shooting. He was one that I had already documented with over the limit of doves.

One of the landowner's sons, John, hollered at the guy, saying, "Come on!" It looked as though everyone was just standing around talking. The hunter responded, "Bet I got over fifty!" John yelled back at him, as he was now through the fence, "Well there's a fellow up here that's gonna count them for you!" Thankfully, John was cooperative and helped defuse the situation. It could easily have gotten out of hand, as all but two hunters had gone over the limit of doves, with the last hunter having the most at fifty-two. I wrote each of them a citation for over the limit, several for unplugged guns, and one for no license.

I placed all the doves in a feed sack and was about to start walking back when John said, "Get on my four-wheeler and I'll carry you back." I gladly took him up on it. John and I were talking as we were heading back, then he made a detour toward the trailer. The women were still on the back porch when we pulled up. John's wife, the one who'd spoken to me earlier, said, "I see you found them." I said, "Yes, ma'am, I did!" John was looking a little confused, as were some of the other hunters who had stopped to get their wives. John said to his wife, "What are you talking about?" She said, "He didn't know where the field was, and I told him how to get there." John, laughing, said, "You told the game warden where we were?" Just about everybody was laughing. John said, kind of laughing, "Oh well, we should've been caught a long time ago." He carried me on to my truck and dropped me off.

We later became good friends, and I got invited to their dove hunts most every year after that, although I didn't ever take them up on the offer. The Patrick family and I are still good friends to this day. They even gave me permission to trap on their property later. I don't believe we meet people by coincidence!

CHAPTER 5

DUCKS IN THE DARKNESS: WHERE'S BOB?

Working on the Mississippi Department of Wildlife, Fisheries, and Parks (law enforcement) waterfowl task force, I was assigned to work the entire waterfowl season with US Fish and Wildlife Service agents. I think our chief at the time did this as punishment, because he wasn't too fond of me! He didn't know I loved it! I truly enjoyed working with Special Agent Robert Oliveri and the other federal agents. We worked Mississippi, Louisiana, and Arkansas in plain clothes and unmarked vehicles. Agent Oliveri and I made numerous waterfowl and dove cases together.

Agent Oliveri and I had been working an area that was loaded with ducks in Yazoo County, Mississippi, along the Yazoo River. One morning, Agent Oliveri and I were driving to Yazoo County to work a place where we had heard a lot of shooting the morning before. We met at 4:00 a.m. at his office in Jackson and then headed that way.

It was looking like a good morning for duck hunting; the temperature was in the mid-thirties with another cold front moving in from the north. Agent Oliveri and I were about thirty minutes away from his office when he spoke, saying that he wasn't feeling well, and I better take him back. I turned around and headed back to his office, dropping him off. I told him that I was going ahead to the area and would try to locate the hunters whom we had heard the morning before. He said, "Let me know what you find."

I again departed for Yazoo County, and it was daylight before I had even reached the spot to begin listening for shots. I pulled over, and, as I got out of the truck, I heard a volley of shots in the same area near the Yazoo River levee. I hopped back in my truck and drove about two miles up the road, where I spotted a truck at the edge of a tree line that snaked through a large bean field. I could see several groups of ducks dropping into the trees. As I rolled my window down, three shots fired, and the ducks came back above the tree line. I thought, "That's got to be our guys!"

I pulled farther down the road until I found a wooded road where I could hide my truck, then hit the edge of a ditch, heading toward the frequent gunfire. As I was getting closer to the truck parked on the edge of the timber, I realized that I was actually hearing two groups of hunters, and the shots closer to me were not nearly as frequent as those on the other side of the slough. I decided to go ahead and try to see who was doing the shooting that was nearest to me.

I slowly passed the truck, and the closer gunfire appeared to be just one hunter, as there were never more than three consecutive shots fired. I continued to slowly walk toward the unknowing hunter. I could see a few decoys, then I noticed ripples in the water coming from someone standing on the other side of a big cypress tree. I squatted in a thick spot, as I could see a large group of ducks coming across the adjoining field. The constant quacking of those big groups of mallards was music to my ears.

The fella behind the cypress tree started calling, and he sounded good! The ducks thought so, too. I could see them starting to cup and circle as they passed over the trees out of my sight. He was calling and kicking the water, causing the ripples that brought his little spread of decoys to life. I then heard the wingbeats of the ducks as they passed over me, very low. Not looking up to keep from flaring the birds, I sat motionless, waiting to see what would take place as the mallards dropped into the trees.

Bam! Bam! Bam! Splash! Splash! Splash! Three shots and three ducks. I started getting a little excited, as I had heard him shoot many times, and the limit of mallards was four. He slowly waded back toward the bank, where he pulled a small jon boat into the water, got in, and paddled to retrieve his downed ducks. I continued to watch and crawled along the edge of the woods until I could see into the boat, about ten yards away. I could see a pile of ducks at the back of the boat, definitely over the limit!

It was getting close to 10:00 a.m., and things were getting slow. He retrieved at least four more ducks. I had belly-crawled under a thick clump of briars and other vegetation close to the boat and within about twenty yards of the hunter. I could tell that he was probably done as he started wading toward the boat. Not wanting to startle him and get shot, I spoke in a normal tone, "Looks like you're having a good hunt." As quick as he saw me, he stepped behind a cypress tree not ten yards away, and I heard several splashes, as if something was being thrown into the water. I quickly spoke again, saying, "Game warden, come out from behind that tree!" He stepped from behind the tree and proceeded toward me. I told him, "Lay your gun down and show me your hunting license and stamps."

He got his wallet out and handed me his hunting license. Mr. Wilson was very nervous as I started counting his ducks; he had ten drake mallards, one hen mallard, and one gadwall. I asked him to empty his pockets so I could see his shotgun shells. He proceeded to empty his shells onto the seat of the aluminum boat. All steel shot. I asked, "What did you throw in the water behind that tree?" He quickly responded, "I didn't throw anything!"

After a brief discussion telling him about his over limit of ducks, I remembered I hadn't checked to see if his gun was plugged. I stepped over and picked up his gun; checking if it was loaded, I shucked out three shells. As I was picking up the shotgun shells, I realized that they were different from the steel shot ones he had shown me earlier. These were all lead shot, Remington #6s to be exact. I knew then what I had heard splash when he stepped behind the tree on me. I questioned him again about it, although it didn't matter because I had the evidence in my hand. He wasn't wanting to talk anymore, so I wrote down his name, address, driver's and hunting license numbers, and phone number and told him that he would be contacted by mail through the US attorney's office. I made a couple of photos of the boat with the pile of ducks, his shotgun, and him. I seized all the ducks and headed to the truck, where I documented violations of over limit and the use of lead shot.

It was nearly noon by the time I got back to the truck. The other shooting had stopped by then. I rode around for several hours trying to locate where the other group had been shooting from but didn't find anything. I made a call to Agent Oliveri and told him about the over limit and lead shot case. He was excited when I told him who it was and said that he'd gotten a tip on that hunter before.

By midafternoon, I hadn't come across anything, so I started toward an area where I knew ducks liked to roost on the Big Black River near Bentonia, also in Yazoo County. At approximately 4:00 p.m., as I was pulled over on Highway 49 near the river, I could see a truck with a dog box in the middle of a soybean field. I decided to get a closer look at the vehicle, thinking it probably was someone deer hunting. I drove out to the truck and saw two empty shotgun shell boxes, both #6 lead shot, and a pair of leather boots.

As I was looking, a volley of shotgun blasts rang out down toward the river. Looking in that direction, I could see a few wood ducks circling back toward the trees. I jumped back in my truck and drove quickly back to the road, parked, grabbed my gear, and headed straight across the open field. I didn't have time to sneak, as it would be dark in less than an hour and I was going to have to work fast to get to the woods and find the shooters before dark.

As I headed across the field as fast as I could walk, blasts from several shotguns were getting more frequent and ducks were starting to steadily fly toward where the shots were coming from. I crossed three sets of boot tracks headed in the direction of the shots, so I followed them. I was racing with the sun as it was falling quickly from the sky. Amazing what a rush of adrenalin you get when things are getting tight!

Ducks were coming from the west consistently—the beautiful orange, red, and blue of the sunset. I was nearing the edge of the woods, and the shotguns were steadily roaring! I was about a hundred yards deep in the woods and could tell I was getting close, as the blasts from the shotguns were getting even louder. The light in the woods was fading fast, so I kept easing toward what sounded like two guns. I could hear that there was another hunter to my right.

I had hip boots on in the ankle-deep water, as I crept very close to the hunters. As a group of woodies came in, a man stepped away from a tree, raising his gun and firing three shots; as he was firing, another guy about twenty yards past him started shooting. The wood ducks and mallards just kept pouring in! The guy I couldn't see was steadily shooting. It was getting so dark, I could see the muzzle flash from their shotguns as they shot at the ducks, determined to land them in the flooded timber.

I stood behind a tree less than twenty yards from the two hunters; all the sunlight had faded away. I could hear them walking toward me, so I kept the big oak between us until they were about five yards away. Speaking sternly as they walked unsuspectingly on the other side of my tree, I said, "Game warden, don't move!" It was like I jumped two rabbits; they took off running toward the other hunter. The chase was on! I was right behind them running through the water; I hollered, "They're running right at you Bob, get 'em!" It was the only thing I could think to do.

They both stopped and I cut my light on, telling them to lean their guns against the tree beside me and stand still. The other hunter I could hear, but I could not see. I hollered, "Don't let that other one get by you, Bob." It had worked once, so I thought I'd try it again. The other guy responded out of the darkness, "I'm coming out!" I hollered again, "Bob, make sure he picks up all those ducks." Oh well, it had worked twice. The hunter I couldn't see yelled out of the darkness, "I can't find one!" I said, "Come to my light, Bob will get that other one."

I could hear the other hunter splashing as he waded through the timber in my direction, finally coming into my light. I could see as he entered the beam of my flashlight that he had a lanyard full of ducks. Telling him to stand with the other two and lean his gun against the tree, I said, "I'm Warden Prince and y'all are shooting after hours; let me see your shells." They each emptied their pockets, and the two who had run wearing hip boots had nothing but lead shot, the same brand and type as the boxes I had seen at the truck. The other hunter was wearing chest waders with duck calls hanging from his neck; he showed me some steel shot. I asked him to take off his vest and, after checking his pockets, found lead shot. On his lanyard he had ten mallards and five wood ducks. The other two had six wood ducks and two mallards. All the guns were plugged. Upon checking their licenses, the two who had run had no duck stamps; the other one had his license and stamps.

As I was writing all their information down, one asked me, "Where's the other guy?" I said, "What are you talking about?" He said, "The one you were hollering at." I just laughed a little and said, "Oh, Bob?" He said, "Yeah." I said, "He's at home, sick." They even managed to laugh a little, considering the circumstances. I took photos of all the evidence (ducks and lead shot) and the hunters. I then explained to them that they would be contacted by the US attorney's office concerning the charges for shooting after hours, having no waterfowl stamps, using lead shot, and being over the limit.

I then headed back toward the field with all the ducks and the other evidence. After getting into my truck, I called Agent Oliveri (Bob), telling him that he had helped me make a heck of a case! He loved it!

CHAPTER 6

THE REAL QUACK!

The duck season was ending. US Fish and Wildlife Service Special Agent Robert Oliveri, Mississippi Game Warden Red Everette, and I were working an area near Holly Bluff, Mississippi, in the Mississippi Delta. On numerous other days during the season, we had heard quite a bit of shooting in the distance but could never locate where the shooters were hunting. The Mississippi Delta can be tricky due to its vast, flat terrain, with numerous old sloughs and river runs, as well as man-made, flooded duck impoundments. Several times we had tried to get to where the shooting was coming from but would get cut off by some type of water body. On this particular day, we had worked another area earlier with no luck, so we decided to see if they were still shooting in this one.

As we pulled off the highway at approximately 10:00 a.m., we could hear consistent shooting in the same area as before. We drove around to another road and dropped off Warden Everette. He was going to walk along a drainage ditch toward the shooting. Agent Oliveri dropped me off in a field across from the drainage ditch to move in the same direction. He drove back around to the highway, parked, and tried making his way toward the shooting in hopes that at least one of us could make it to the hunters because we could still hear shooting.

Warden Everette said over his radio, "I found two trucks and see two guys on an ATV coming out." Agent Oliveri responded, "Just watch them. I'm getting close to where they are shooting." I was getting closer but still couldn't see anything. Warden Everette said, "They put some ducks in one of the vehicles and are heading back toward the blind; I'll stay close to the vehicles." The shooting was getting slow as I came into sight of the waterhole they were hunting. Agent Oliveri said, "I can see them. It looks like they are getting ready to leave. I'll follow them to the vehicle." I continued toward the blind as I could see it through the trees. I found one breasted duck and one that appeared to have been discarded. Warden Everette had hunters who were coming to their truck and Agent Oliveri wasn't far behind them, so I stated that I was headed their way also.

When I arrived at the truck, Agent Oliveri and Warden Everette had gathered the six hunters in a group and were conducting a routine check of licenses, guns, and ducks. They didn't have over the limit in their possession, and nobody claimed the breasted duck. They did have their ducks in a pile, but when we had them separate the ducks, there was a limit for each person. Also, there was one young college-age girl and another young fellow whom we doubted had shot their limit, but we couldn't prove it. Agent Oliveri scolded them about not having the ducks separated, but he didn't charge them with anything. They were being very sarcastic, almost as if they knew they had beaten us. We suspected that they had done something, but it didn't appear we were going to find anything.

One young man with a video camera was walking around videoing and narrating, "The game wardens are checking us." He was laughing during his narration. I asked the young man politely to stop videoing me. He laughed. I walked over to Agent Oliveri and said, "Let's seize his videotape." Agent Oliveri said, "Do it!" I told the young man that I wanted the tape from his camera. His response was quick: "You can't do that!" I told him that due to the pile of ducks, the breasted duck, and the duck I'd found near the blind, we were going to seize the tape and would get it back to him after we viewed it. I asked him to remove the tape or we would take both the tape and the camera: "Make it light on yourself!" He looked as though he knew this was not good; the whole hunting party looked as though they had seen a ghost, and things got very quiet! After he handed me the tape, I gave him a receipt for it and told him that we would be getting back in touch with him after viewing it.

After we returned to the office that night, we realized why they were so scared. We never expected that the tape would have so much evidence on it. He had taped several hunts, with dates and times, that were definitely over the limits. We were able to identify many of the hunters, but we were going to have to do several follow-up interviews with each individual. One part of the video showed footage at the home of the videographer's uncle, Mr. Cannon. During the video, Mr. Cannon's wife counted out forty-eight mallards and made the comment, "Oh my, good thing the game warden didn't check y'all!"

After follow-up interviews, we charged six individuals with multiple Migratory Bird Treaty Act violations. All individuals charged pled guilty, with monetary fines in the thousands of dollars and two individuals losing hunting privileges. That video told the story and made our case!

CHAPTER 7

CHASING A FRIEND: ILLEGAL NETS

The Ross Barnett Reservoir was closed to all commercial fishing, and one of the best commercial fishermen on the water was my target. Normally the commercial guys would run nets late at night. It was a game of cat and mouse. I didn't have much help from other wardens when it came to chasing commercial fishermen around, but I loved sitting out on the water until the wee hours of the morning, waiting to hear a net being pulled. It was a great time to be with God to enjoy the majesty of His creation on those nights when the heavens are filled with stars.

Nothing sounds quite like the "clank, clank, clank" of the lead on the bottom of the nets being pulled into an aluminum boat and hitting the sides. Also, the sound of a large catfish or buffalo flopping around in the boat is distinctive. Those sounds could be heard from quite a distance. We made many illegal commercial cases, but one fisherman, Carroll, was a regular. He and I had actually become friends over the years, after I'd caught him and seized his nets numerous times. It had gotten to where I would just tell Carroll to go by my house and get his nets after he paid his fines. Carroll just said it was the cost of doing business.

One night I had a young officer named Donald in the boat with me. It was one of those nights when everything was perfect—the wind was calm, there was no boat traffic, and the stars gave one a good view on the water. The hum of an outboard in the distance got my adrenaline pumping, as there were no lights visible—the first sign of something illegal! As the hum died out minutes later, the first "clank" might have been a drag, then came the steady "clank, clank, clank." I whispered to Donald, with a big smile on my face, "That's a net."

Donald was anxious about his first commercial fishing case and kept asking, "When?" I said to wait and let him move closer, as he was not visible. As we heard the hum of the outboard again, Donald said, "He's going the other way!" I said that he would come back. Donald said, "He's going to get away!" Against my better judgment, I fired up the forty horsepower on the fourteen-foot aluminum boat and headed that way, running without lights. As long as Carroll's boat was running, he couldn't hear, but the same went for us! We hit the channel and planed out at full speed. With a forty-horsepower outboard motor on a fourteen-foot-long, five-foot-wide aluminum boat, she would fly!

Suddenly I could have slapped Carroll, as we barely missed hitting him head on! Carroll's eyes were as wide as saucers! The chase was on, with no lights going on either boat. If a light were turned on, it would mess up our night vision; best to run blacked out. Carroll knew the lake better than most of the fish and I knew it just about as well. I kept trying to follow him by crossing his wake, but eventually he escaped. I cut my boat off, hoping to hear Carroll's, but I figured that Carroll was in the stumps sitting quietly, waiting on us to leave. It was an exciting night, but Carroll won, as he had many times before.

The following morning at the local café and bait shop, where most of the fishermen and hunters generally met to share their stories, I was sitting drinking a cup of coffee when Carroll walked in and made his way to the coffeepot. When Carroll spotted me, he hesitated, then came over to my table and asked, "Mind if I sit down?" I nodded, sure. Many in the restaurant who knew Carroll were in disbelief as they saw him sit with the game warden!

After taking a long sip on his coffee, he looked over at me with a long smirky grin and said, "That was kinda close last night!" We both laughed and finished drinking our coffee. It was kind of like the cartoon with the sheepdog and the coyote years ago, when they would sit and talk, then go their different ways to do their job!

On another occasion, at about 9:00 p.m., I saw Carroll and an unknown individual gassing their boat at a service station near the Ross Barnett Reservoir. No doubt where they were headed! If I was right, they would probably launch their boat at Fannin Landing. I sped away, hoping they hadn't spotted me, and hid my truck on an old logging road near the landing. As I neared the opening close to the boat ramp, I heard the unmistakable sound of a truck and trailer fast approaching. The two commercial fishermen unloading the boat were like a highly trained Coast Guard unit in their speed. No telling how many times they had backed a boat, unhooked, and launched, as they took maybe a minute, two at the most!

I recognized Carroll but not the individual who was driving the truck. Carroll had backed the boat off into the darkness of the lake, killing the motor, while the other subject parked the vehicle in the woods out of sight. Carroll eased to the bank, the unknown man jumped in, and they sped away across the lake into the darkness.

I could not see them, but when the motor would go quiet, I could hear the unmistakable clanking of net weights and fish flopping in the darkness. I knew they were far from being caught and was trying to decide how I was going to contact them. If anything spooked Carroll before they got the boat back on the trailer, he would just take off into the darkness, getting rid of any illegal nets and fish they possessed.

If they did what I expected, the one driving the truck would back the trailer into the water as the boat operator was driving the boat onto the trailer, all in one motion. By the time the boat hit the bow roller on the trailer, the driver would be pulling away from the launch, not stopping until they were at a safe location far away from the landing, with the boat operator staying in the boat until then.

I eased to their truck and slid in the back. The bed of the truck was full of clutter, and it was easy to cover myself with an old tarp they were probably going to use to cover their fish. What I was doing was not in the playbooks, but as most game wardens did to apprehend subjects, I was going to push it.

I could hear the boat approach the shore, then reverse and quiet. The sound of quick footsteps approaching was hard to hear over my heartbeat. What a rush! So far, so good, as the truck cranked, circled into the parking area, and backed into the launch. It worked just as I had expected—not that it always did.

The truck never stopped running, but I could hear the outboard, the bump as the boat hit the trailer, the throttle opening up, and a clank as the bow hit the front roller. Things were getting exciting as the truck started pulling away from the landing and I eased up and hit the cab's roof with my flashlight shouting, "Stop, game warden!"

The sudden stop of the truck almost threw me over the cab! As quickly as the truck stopped, the unknown subject exited as I jumped from the back. This person immediately assumed a threatening demeanor as I told him to place his hands on the truck. The situation was escalating quickly, and I didn't even know where the other person was located.

Carroll's familiar voice suddenly shouted to the individual: "Shut up and do what he says!" I turned as Carroll stepped between me and the unknown subject, then stepped back as he calmed his partner. Carroll told him to stay at the truck as he turned to me. With a grin on his face, he said, "That was a good one!" Carroll told the guy to unload the fish and nets and to not say anything.

I issued them both a citation for illegal commercial fishing, telling Carroll that he could have the nets when he paid the ticket. He shook my hand before leaving. I learned later that the unknown man was a convicted felon who had recently gotten out of prison for holding a man while another stabbed him to death. I thanked Carroll later for not letting that situation go bad.

The friendship between Carroll and me grew in the years to come. He didn't live far from me, and I invited him to go to church. Much to my surprise, he started coming to church, accepted Christ, and was baptized. Yep, wouldn't have thought it, but God opens doors even in the strangest of relationships. Amazing how God works!

Carroll taught me a lot about the illegal commercial market that was beneficial later in my career of working covertly in the Special Operations Unit. Carroll gave up these activities himself, due primarily to his health. He showed me how and where a lot of the illegally caught fish were sold, as I posed as his helper. We had a unique friendship that lasted until Carroll went to be with the Lord.

CHAPTER 8

HIGH-SPEED HEADLIGHTERS

Many outlaws will poach deer at night with a spotlight. This type of activity is often called headlighting. On one headlighting detail, the same young game warden I described working with in the previous chapter, Donald, was working with me. He had told me after the boat ride chasing Carroll that he was not getting back in a boat with me! Ha! That might have been a little too much for him! No boats this time. Two other wardens were set up in the area we were working. There were a lot of dairy cattle in that location, so we were working complaints about shots being fired late at night near ryegrass fields where the cattle fed.

It was a warm night for December, so Donald and I were sitting on the toolbox in the back of the truck. The night was very dark, and the only noise was that of the radio dispatch calling out complaints to officers across the state. About 1:00 a.m., we saw a glow coming down the road with the sound of crunching gravel following the light of the vehicle, moving very slowly.

Donald and I were set up where the road made a ninety-degree turn at the entrance to a large, green field; it was a perfect spot to swing the headlights of a vehicle across the unsuspecting deer. As the vehicle approached, it was evident that they were up to something. When it came to the curve, the brake lights came on; something was about to happen, and our adrenalin was pumping. Donald and I knew that the possible poachers were looking at a deer because we put it there! The full-body mounted deer we called Rudolph had apprehended many poachers already, and it looked as though he was about to take another bullet for wildlife conservation. We couldn't see exactly what they were doing due to the brush; tensions built as it seemed time stood still.

Then, the unmistakable crack—*kaaaabooom*—of their high-caliber firearm broke the stillness of the night.

We were in the truck, with blue lights and siren blaring, in a high-speed chase within seconds. As quickly as things were happening, on a gravel road at sixty-five to seventy miles per hour, I forgot the road had a *T* around the curve. We drove trucks, which were not made to chase cars! About the time I remembered the *T*, we were airborne! Thankfully, the field we went aerial into had no trees or fencing along the road.

I could hear Donald let out some type of scream or prayer, all in the same garbled noise. Fortunately, we landed on all four tires and got back in pursuit. The poachers were gone, either wrecked or hiding, as we turned off blue lights and siren, then notified the other officers by radio to look for the vehicle by the best description we could give. No tag number, make, or model of vehicle, just a big car. Kind of hard to see much but taillights on that dusty, gravel road. They got away, but it had been a rush! I asked Donald if he was okay, as he had gotten kind of quiet. He uttered a few choice words aimed at me and my driving, and seemed a bit shaken as we pulled back into the setup location.

I told Donald to stay at the truck while I checked on Rudolph. As I walked the gravel road toward the field, I thought I saw a figure cross the road in the darkness. I slipped back to the truck, told Donald what I had seen, and grabbed the Remington 870 shotgun and a light. I told Donald to skirt the road on the edge of the woods as I circled the subject.

I went several hundred yards through the woods (with no lights) and circled back toward the road. As I slowly approached the road, I could make out the silhouette of a man at the edge of the road. I crept closer and closer, each step slowly and solidly planted, until reaching the cover of a small tree. With nothing else between us, I racked the 870, cutting on the flashlight and shouting at the same moment, "Hands up, game warden!" The subject was startled but did as he was told. Donald came and assisted as I was handcuffing the subject to escort him back to the truck.

The subject was a man in his early twenties. As we questioned him, he denied shooting at a deer, saying that he had just been dropped off by some friends. Not knowing even the name of the road he was standing in as he was questioned, he finally admitted that he had stepped out of the vehicle to shoot deer, and when we cranked up, his buddies left him standing in the road. I told Donald that they would be back and we would be waiting. The young man was pretty shaken; I offered him some coffee and made him sit in the truck.

About an hour later, a vehicle different from the one we had chased slowly came down the road. I said that had to be them. As I stepped into the road with my flashlight pointed at the vehicle, it stopped. I was holding the 870, and asked the driver to turn the truck engine off and get out of the vehicle. He slowly exited the vehicle, being totally cooperative. His first words were that he was looking for his son.

I told him that his son was at the truck and the normal procedure was to take him to jail. I thought as he walked to the truck that it was getting close to Christmas, and now his son was doing something as stupid as headlighting. I spoke to the young man sternly as I removed the cuffs, "Going to give your daddy a break, not you!" I escorted the young man to his father and told the man to take care of him and to have a Merry Christmas! The man was grateful, shaking my hand. He turned to his son, and it was evident by the look he gave him as he climbed in the truck, he might have come out better going to jail!

CHAPTER 9

OFFICER UNDER FIRE!

I received some information concerning a "trophy poacher" whom I had spent many long nights trying to apprehend. The informant was a good source, as I had made many cases off his tips before. He had overheard the old poacher I had been after, bragging about how he had been outsmarting the game wardens over the years, and he used my name in particular. That got under my skin even more. He said that he would be glad to put some holes in me if I ever stopped him.

I called Donald, the young warden who had been working headlighting activities with me, to see if he wanted to work that night. He seemed a little reluctant, considering the high-speed boat chase we had been on the week before, but agreed anyway. He probably could tell I was excited about the information I had received. I told him I would pick him up about 8:00 p.m.

After picking up Donald, we headed toward an area called Pelahatchie, a rural area checkerboarded with agriculture and poultry farms. There were lots of deer in the area, and the cornfields that lined the roads made for a poacher's paradise. We tried to use as many backroads as possible to reach the area without bumping into any traffic. There were plenty of guys who knew this old poacher, and they would alert him if they saw a game warden's truck in the area.

As we were approaching our setup location, I hit the toggle switch under my dash that cut off all lights on the vehicle. It's amazing how far you can see brake lights in the distance, and we didn't want to take a chance on spooking our target. I pointed to a little hill in the large cornfield to our right. I told Donald that we would set up in the small cluster of pecan trees on that hill, as we would be able to see three different county roads, a good spot.

As I saw a vehicle in the distance coming our way, I sped up to make the turn in the field without being noticed. Donald said, "There's a vehicle in the field under the trees." I was focused on the oncoming vehicle's headlights when Donald said: "There's two vehicles under the trees and someone is getting out of one!"

This was the point when the world of law enforcement diverged from normal activities, when vision tunneled and events seemingly went into slow motion. I took a glance and said, "Probably some kids parking." I quickly tried to focus on the oncoming vehicle, as I wanted to make sure it wasn't our target. We were off the road and hidden from the oncoming headlights.

Donald, still watching the parked cars, said, "He's getting something out of the other vehicle." The vehicles were on the horizon from the vantage point of our position at the bottom of the hill. I took another glance back at the parked vehicles on the hill and then tried to look back for the oncoming vehicle. Donald excitedly yelled out, "He's got a gun!"

By the time I focused on a man silhouetted on the horizon in the stillness of the night, fire seemed to light up the darkness, followed by a loud *ka-boom*! I hit blue lights, grabbed the mic on the radio, and hollered, "Officer under fire!" (no location given), dropping the mic and putting the truck in reverse all in the same motion. It sounded like shot was spraying the front of the truck.

The radio message went out across the county, with numerous officers hearing it, but they were unable to respond due to lack of a location. As the call was going out, the individual who had fired got into his vehicle and started down the hill toward us. I told Donald, "Grab the 870!" Not looking at him, I heard the distinct sound of the Remington 870 shotgun racking a round of .00 buckshot into the chamber.

As Donald leveled over the passenger door, I took a position through the frame of the truck door and the windshield. I had my Smith & Wesson .357 ready as the vehicle stopped less than twenty yards away. Thankfully, he stopped directly in the headlights of my vehicle, as I had already tightened my grip on that .357. I recognized the individual (it was the landowner!) as he was getting out, and I started yelling, "Blake, get your hands up!" Thank God he did, as both Donald and I were starting to squeeze the triggers on our weapons!

As Blake staggered to the front of his vehicle with hands up and no weapon, I placed him in a prone position and got him cuffed. Donald grabbed the weapon out of his truck and unloaded it. The adrenaline rush of the moment was unbelievable, as I continued to ask Blake, "Are you crazy? What are you doing, you stupid fool?" In his drunken state, he garbled out, "I thought you were Joe." I responded, "Joe who?" Blake quietly said, with his face still in the gravel, "Her husband!"

I was still confused and so angry, I just wanted to beat the snot out of him! I left him lying on the cold ground with only his pants on, while I defused the situation I had started on the radio. I told dispatch, "Everything is OK, subject is in custody." I returned to Blake and, with a very angry tone, continued to belittle him as he lay on the ground. "We almost killed you, you idiot!" He said, "I just shot over you!" I said, "You knew I was going to be working this area, I asked about parking here!" He held his head low and started apologizing. I said, "You are an idiot, and one day someone's probably going to kill you for fooling with their wife, you're just stupid!"

I took the cuffs off him and allowed him to put a coat on as I contemplated what to do. We had a justifiable assault arrest, but the biggest kink was, it was Blake's property. I told Donald that we were going to call it a night. I looked over at Blake and again told him how close we'd come to killing him. I looked at Donald and said, "Let's go."

We drove several miles before either of us said a word, as the rush of what had just taken place was beginning to wear off. Donald said, "I'm not sure I want to do this." I responded, "What do you mean?" He didn't answer. He was pretty shaken and so was I. I dropped him off at his home, and that was the last game warden detail he worked. Several days later, the chief of law enforcement for the agency told me that Donald had transferred, turning in his badge and gun. Donald went to work in the fisheries division. He just got in on too much, too quickly. I guess it was best. Not everyone is cut out for this kind of work!

CHAPTER 10

GOING UNDER: TRANSFERRING TO SPECIAL OPS

I had been working for the Mississippi Department of Wildlife, Fisheries, and Parks since early 1983, with many investigations under my belt (both overt and light covert). The last fifteen years of my career, I worked in the covert unit (special operations—i.e., deep cover). Very few people knew what I actually did for a living. Many rumors were spread that I had been fired and was just working odd jobs and trapping.

The depth of the covert position is such that no uniformed officer was to acknowledge a special operations agent if they made contact in public. After some time in deep cover, my physical appearance had changed so much that I was checked in the field by officers whom I had worked with in uniform, and they didn't recognize me, since my hair was now on my shoulders and my ungroomed beard further changed my appearance. The position was not like what most people see on television; there was nothing glamorous.

During my time working as an undercover agent, I saw many agents come and go. Only a few stuck with it, as it is hard on family life, with many days away from home without contact with family. Most of those who thought they wanted to work as a covert agent rarely stayed very long.

The positions within the Special Operations Unit are all deep cover, even the supervisor. When someone joins that unit, everything that person does is confidential, for the integrity of the case and the safety of the agent(s). It takes people with patience and a special personality to work in a covert wildlife position, as well as a special dedication to the job. Unlike other covert positions such as narcotics, a covert wildlife officer normally works alone, just checking in periodically with the case agent or supervisor to report the work location—where they would be going—as well as report any new contacts the

This is another guided fishing trip (undercover). (Photo courtesy of the MDWFP.)

officer may have encountered. All contacts with subjects under investigation are recorded (audio and video when possible). Agents sometimes work jointly on large investigations. Many hours are spent doing reports, as each contact must be included in a report.

On-the-Job Training

In law enforcement, most specialized positions normally require some type of training. I never went to any schools to learn covert work. It was all on-the-job training. I did have a good relationship with Assistant US Attorney John Dowdy, who explained to me what I needed to take a case to federal court as well as how he wanted a case documented. Special Agent Robert Oliveri with the US Fish and Wildlife Service was also very influential in my growth in covert wildlife investigations. He was in charge of Mississippi, Louisiana, and Arkansas. I spent a lot of time working with agents of the Bureau of Alcohol, Tobacco, and Firearms (ATF) as well as agents of the FBI.

I started out working on cases such as guided hunts or fishing trips, where I would pay an individual to take me hunting. I would document violations committed by the guides and/or others in the group (hunters and/or fishermen). Those cases rarely lasted more than a couple of days and were relatively easy to work.

I also worked on other, smaller investigations, such as local Indian powwows across the state. Normally these cases involved the illegal sale of some type of wild animal parts (eagle and other raptor feathers and claws, antlers, and bones used to make Indian artifacts) and narcotics (mostly marijuana). Most of the individuals who were charged in these cases were card-carrying members of tribes but were less Indian than I, and my great-grandmother was full blooded! They were trying to make money off Native American privileges (Native Americans can possess certain items for rituals, but it is illegal to sell such items). The biggest case we had involved the purchase of a mounted eagle. An individual we met at a powwow in Brandon, Mississippi, talked about having a mounted golden eagle he wanted to sell. The individual was from Arkansas. We set up the deal in Greenwood, Mississippi. We did a "buy-bust" on the individual, and he was charged with a federal violation of the Lacey Act as well as the illegal sale of the eagle for $500.

During my fifteen years working undercover, my cover was only jeopardized twice—both times by a law enforcement officer. One knowingly identified me to warn a friend, and the other just made a bad decision.

CHAPTER 11

CHASING HOME BOYS IN THE BITTERROOT MOUNTAINS

The Mississippi Special Operations Unit received a call from an investigator at Idaho Fish and Game concerning possible illegal hunting activity by Mississippi hunters in Idaho. They had gotten information through a hotline tip that hunters were coming from Mississippi to Idaho, illegally killing elk and deer, then transporting them back to Mississippi. They wanted us to try to covertly contact an Idaho resident, Bo Reeves, who had moved there from Mississippi. He was supposedly guiding without a license, assuming he was charging a fee, for friends from Mississippi.

Mississippi only had two covert agents at the time, David King and me. Agent King had not been working very long but was a very good investigator. We decided to work a joint investigation with Idaho Fish and Game, along with Special Agent Robert Oliveri of the US Fish and Wildlife Service. The Idaho agency would cover all costs such as travel, food, and licenses.

The gun season for elk opened in mid-October, so we planned a two-week trip and booked a motel close to where Bo Reeves lived. Our plan was to stay in a little community up in the panhandle of Idaho. We drove to Idaho from Mississippi in two days, which was a long trip in a single-cab truck! In Boise, we met with Investigator Mike Rogers, who had contacted us earlier regarding the alleged illegal activities and got directions to the motel. Rogers had driver's license photographs of Bo and his brother Matt Reeves, who was from Mississippi. I glanced at the photographs and realized that Matt was wearing a Mississippi law enforcement uniform. This was not good; I didn't want to investigate a law enforcement officer, but if he was doing what they said, he needed to be stopped. Investigator Rogers stated that Matt had been out hunting several times over the years and had only purchased a small-game license. He also gave us a description and tag number of the truck that Bo drove.

After receiving the information, I asked the investigator about us shooting game during the course of the investigation to maintain cover. He said, "We would prefer you don't kill anything." I was thinking, Mississippi boys don't miss much, but I didn't say anything. After a little more discussion, Investigator Rogers stated that there was an antigovernment group in that area. I thought, "Well, that's good to know." I said that we would do our best to document any illegal activity, and we headed out.

We had about a four-hour drive from Boise straight north into the panhandle of Idaho, some beautiful but rugged country. The drive started off very enjoyably, as the mountains are amazingly beautiful, but just after sundown the weather started to change, and it began raining heavily. We were on some very steep, curvy mountain roads, and I had seen signs to watch for falling rocks, when I noticed brake lights starting to show on several vehicles up the road. With a loud *bam*, the front left tire blew as I hit falling rocks!

We got off the road as best we could; considering the incline, it was not a good place to change a tire! There were plenty of rocks to chock the truck with, but the heavy rainfall made a bad situation even worse. The tire was split, so now we were going to have to find a place to buy a tire in the middle of nowhere. After getting the tire changed, we continued, cold and wet, finally making it to the little motel not far from where our target lived. Thankfully, there was someone there to check us in, considering we were over an hour late.

We got checked in and had no trouble going to sleep. The next morning, we asked where we could find a tire, as we definitely needed a spare. The fellow who owned the eight-room motel and attached store selling groceries, fuel, and hunting supplies gave us directions to get a tire. As best as I could tell, there was no one but hunters at the motel. It took us about half a day to get a tire and back in our target area. We did a drive-by at Bo Reeves's home and saw a vehicle that matched the description of the one in our files. At least we were at a starting point.

Now came the toughest part of wildlife undercover work, contacting the target! David and I drove around quite a bit the first day, enjoying the scenery. The mountains and rivers running through the valleys were beautiful! We took a lot of pictures, but there was no way to trap that kind of beauty in the lens of my little 35 mm camera. We saw quite a few deer, mostly whitetails and a few mule deer, but no elk.

Later in the evening, we parked off the road coming from Bo Reeves's home and decided to just wait and see if he drove by headed to the store, but to no avail. We went back to the store after dark and shopped around a little, talking with some of the other hunters who were staying at the motel. One group was actually from Mississippi, but nothing indicated that they were hunting with our target, as they had brought horses, and from the information we had received, Bo and those who hunted with him primarily hunted from the road.

The next morning, we got up before daylight, went in the store, and stayed around drinking coffee as long as we could without looking suspicious. We decided to head out before the sun came up and at least appear that we were hunting. We drove farther into the Bitterroot Mountains to the Panhandle National Forest. As we were driving, still before daylight, a large herd of elk crossed the road in front of us.

We pulled farther up the road and got out to see if there was a bull in the group. The sun was just beginning to break through the thick lodgepole pines and give enough light to ease through the timber. As we were slipping along, we heard the unmistakable whistle and grunting of a bugling elk down farther through the timber. That got my blood pumping! I got my diaphragm turkey call from my pocket and bugled back at him. I had guided elk hunts in Colorado for several years when I was in college. He responded, and I could tell that he didn't like the challenge. I made a cow call. He responded again and was closer. David and I sat down by a large rock outcropping and just waited to see what would happen.

Within five minutes, we could see a couple of cows sneaking toward us. The next bugle blew my hat off as I saw the bull's massive six-by-six crown slowly working toward us through the timber. He was awesome! He continued to within thirty yards, but we had not been watching the cows that had passed through the trees and gotten behind us. One of the cows winded us and spooked, as the cold mountain air was carrying our scent up the mountain behind us. She trotted down toward the meadow, with the other elk following. The bull just watched as if, "Where you gals going?" He slowly turned and followed his harem out of sight into the meadow below.

We gave them a few minutes, then followed them until we could see the entire herd about a hundred yards away in a meadow. There were two smaller bulls with the big six-by-six, but they were staying clear from him, not challenging his authority. I couldn't stand it; I took my rifle and put the cross hairs behind the big bull's shoulder. As I was scoping him, his knees buckled, and *bam*! At first, I thought I'd shot him (hard to do without a loaded gun)! Gunfire continued to ring out, echoing across the meadow to our right, as both the smaller bulls were also shot.

The three bulls were all down, and I could see three hunters making their way down toward the meadow. David and I went down, congratulated them, and admired that massive six-by-six; he was a trophy to say the least, a Boone and Crockett record book bull. Well, we enjoyed the hunt, but those guys were about to have to pack a lot of meat out, along with antlers. We left, but I'm sure they were there 'til dark.

It was time for us to head back to town and see if we could bump into our target, so we left. As we rounded the curve, we could see what appeared to be our target's vehicle at the store's gas pump. We pulled up to the gas pump on the other side, between the store and the pumps. Hopefully, he would notice our Mississippi tag and speak to us, which would make things easier. I noticed our target when he exited the store. He walked right past the back of our truck, and bingo! He glanced at the license plate on our truck and did a double take. I was pumping gas and acted as though I wasn't paying him any attention.

As he stepped around the pump to his truck, he paused and said, "You guys from Mississippi?" I responded, "Yeah, we trying to do a little hunting." He said, "What y'all after?" I said, "We got deer and elk tags but haven't had much luck." He said, "There's plenty up in these parts." He continued with, "I used to live in Mississippi near Tupelo." I asked how he wound up in Idaho. Bo said, "I came out here to work at the hydroelectric dams and just loved it, so I moved here." We continued with our discussion. He was very cordial and gave me his phone number, saying, "If y'all need anything, give me a call." Not wanting to jump too quickly, we told him thanks and that we hoped to see him again. He got into his truck and offered a little help by giving us directions to a hunting area that, according to him, would be a good place. He then drove off.

Well, at least we had made contact. He seemed mostly at ease with us, but I suspected he would give his brother our tag number and check us out. Thankfully, the tag was registered under my covert name and address in Mississippi. We left the store and went to the area he had told us about along the Clearwater River. Once there, we gathered our hunting gear and hiked until we found a meadow, and just like any other hunters, we sat and glassed for elk. Another full day and we were exhausted; it was no problem sleeping that night.

The next morning was the same routine, except that a front was coming in and it started to snow. It was beautiful, and for two guys from Mississippi, not a regular sight. We drove back up into the mountains, where we saw a camp with horses, two large wall tents, and several vehicles, including a truck and horse trailer. We stopped to talk with whoever was at the camp, mainly just killing time, then bumped into a rough-looking character who introduced himself as Bryan Smith.

We talked hunting for a bit, and when we told him where we were from, he said, "I used to live in Biloxi, Mississippi." I almost laughed, saying, "You're kidding!" He said he used to be a registered nurse and worked at the hospital

Our base camp in the Bitterroot Mountains in the panhandle of Idaho. (Photo courtesy of the MDWFP.)

in Biloxi. We continued to talk; he told us he was now an outfitter and had a group of hunters that he was going to get the following day. After further conversation, he offered for us to spend the night and go with him to pick up the hunters he had at a spike camp about four hours on horseback into the mountains. After he asked if we could ride horses, it appeared he was looking for some help. He said, "You can bring your rifles and if we bump into an elk you can shoot it and I'll pack it out." That sounded good to me, as we had camping gear and sleeping bags in the truck. We grabbed our gear, carried it into the big wall tent, and had a small supper of canned food.

We enjoyed the conversation throughout the night, as our new friend was definitely an outlaw, even if only half of what he said was true! He spoke of poaching alligators in Mississippi, and the best part of one of his stories was what he said made the best gator bait. He said, "I worked in the labor and delivery section of the hospital, and one of my jobs was to take the placenta and umbilical cord and after a certain number of days they were to be incinerated. I would put them in a plastic bag and walk right out the front door of the hospital. Great alligator bait." Wow, never heard that one before. This guy is nuts!

I found out the following morning that my partner may have exaggerated about his experience with horses. Although he said he had ridden horses, he undoubtedly had never saddled one! Oh well! After getting my horse saddled

Headed into the mountains to pick up hunters. (Photo courtesy of the MDWFP.)

up, I went over to help David, as he didn't know how to tie a girth. I didn't say anything since I didn't want to embarrass him, but I could tell when he mounted up, he hadn't spent many hours on a horse. I was excited as we headed out, each of us leading a string of packhorses. I told David, "Watch your rifle in this timber, because if it catches a tree, that could snatch it out of the scabbard." He was holding the saddle horn pretty tight as we snaked our way through the heavy timber.

When we made it to the spike camp, Bryan was not happy when he saw that the hunters were not packed up and ready to go; they said they had an elk down in a meadow over the next ridge. We went with Bryan and the hunters to the downed elk. It was a pretty steep hill; I told Bryan that I could ride my horse down with the packhorse. The steep grade was tough as my horse was squatting and sliding, and I kicked him to make him head down toward the meadow. David, Bryan, and the hunters just walked down, leaving their horses on the ridge. Bryan and I quartered the elk and placed it on the packhorse. I then caped out the head, as they wanted to mount it. We then fixed the head and rack on my horse and started back up. We had a load!

When we made it back to the spike camp, Bryan told them to get packed up, that we were heading out! I didn't say anything, but the clouds were moving in, the temperature was dropping, and there was no way we could get back to the base camp in just a couple of hours. It would be at least six hours—that is, if we could get packed up quickly. Oh well, he was determined to head back. The party was four hunters, one of whom was a woman. By the time we got packed, it was starting to snow heavily.

We all got mounted up, with Bryan taking the lead. The wind and snow were tough, to say the least, as we made it to the top of the first ridge. The woman was complaining about the cold, so we stopped, wrapped her legs with garbage bags, and continued. I honestly believed that Bryan would leave them, as he would get a good distance out of sight, and by now it was black dark with the snow literally blowing uphill as we got back into the thick timber. I thought, this guy is nuts! David was behind me, and I told him to hop off his horse and walk a little to get some blood flowing to help warm him up; he wouldn't. I also reminded him to keep checking his rifle. He wasn't responding much. That was one long ride; we made it back to base camp just before daylight. We all went into the big wall tent, where there was a little wood heater. I started shucking clothes; woman or not, I wanted dry clothes. I had laid my rifle in the corner of the tent and didn't notice that David hadn't, as I wanted to get in my sleeping bag and grab a little shut-eye. Even with all the talk, I quickly fell asleep.

A couple of hours later I awoke, and the hunters were gone. David was sitting in the corner sipping on some coffee Bryan had made. I quickly grabbed some and asked, "Where's Bryan?" David said, "He's loading horses or something." I could tell something was bothering him, so I asked if he was okay. He responded, "I lost my rifle on the way back." I was a little harsh, saying, "I told you those trees were going to snatch it out if you didn't keep a check on it!" I didn't need to say anything else, as I wasn't making things better. It was a 7 mm with a nice Leupold scope. We told Bryan, but he was quick to say, "There's no way to find it in all of that fresh snow." I'm sure Bryan went back and found it after the snow melted. Of course he wouldn't call if he did. I didn't tell David what I was thinking, but I'm pretty sure he could read my mind, as he didn't say much after we left camp and made our way back to the motel.

The following day, we bumped into Bo again at the store and had a brief conversation about our hunt. He was very talkative but said he had to work the next couple of days. He did tell us, if we ever decided to come back, to give him a call beforehand and he would help us. Didn't look like we were going to get anywhere on this trip, but we did have a good contact and things were looking good for the following year.

After a couple more days of riding around, we decided to head back to Boise. About halfway there, we contacted Investigator Rogers and informed him of what had transpired. He was excited, and we decided to meet at a hotel in Boise. That night in Boise, we met, returned our tags and license, and told him about our contacts with Bo and the outfitter, Bryan. We told him that after we returned we would do a full report and email it to him. He asked, "Think y'all could try it again next year?" I said, "We'll see, but we are definitely going to fly next time and just rent a vehicle." He said, "Great, let's do it!"

We spent the night in Boise and drove straight through back to Mississippi! During the next several months, David made several calls to Bo, just trying to stay in contact about possibly going back out there hunting. He never mentioned a fee but said that his brother and a friend were coming out the following season, so maybe we could go hunting with them. Bingo, just what we needed to hear. David notified Investigator Rogers, and we started planning another trip. Idaho Fish and Game would fly us out and rent us a four-wheel-drive truck.

It wasn't long before we were headed back to Idaho. At least this time we wouldn't be exhausted when we got there! David had talked to Bo, and he told us the dates his brother Matt was coming and that he would be off work. He told David to just give him a call and let him know when we got there. The wheels were turning, and things were looking good.

After we flew into Boise, Investigator Rogers picked us up in the four-wheel-drive truck he'd rented, with all our licenses (big game and small game) and tags. Bo had told David we might do some grouse hunting. During a brief meeting, he told us that Matt and Jesse McDaniel, who was also from Mississippi, had each purchased a nonresident small game license but no elk or deer license. Well, we knew they would be in violation if they killed anything other than upland birds or small game.

After our long drive from Boise to the motel near Elk City, David gave Bo a call, and he invited us to his place, giving us directions on how to get there from the motel. Bo said, "Y'all come about lunch and we'll go shoot some grouse later." The following morning, David and I did a last-minute check on our microcassette tape recorders, as we wanted to make sure we got everything on tape.

We headed to Bo's house and, as usual on a first contact, got butterflies in our stomachs, especially with his brother Matt being a twenty-year law enforcement officer! Years earlier when I was a uniformed game warden I had taught classes at the Mississippi Law Enforcement Training Academy. I had met a lot of law enforcement officers, hopefully not Matt! As we pulled into the long, graveled drive, David cut his recorder on and prefaced it with date, time, and location. We didn't say anything else until we got out of the truck and introduced ourselves.

Bo greeted us, introducing us to his brother and Jesse McDaniel. We all ate lunch together and told hunting stories. During the conversation, I realized that Matt was Jesse's supervisor; he was a law enforcement officer as well. Bo said, "Let's go kill some grouse!" He loaned David and me a shotgun each and a box of shells. We stepped off the back porch and headed across the field to a wooded draw behind Bo's house. As we were walking across the field, we could see what appeared to be a deer hanging in a little barn at the edge of the field.

We slowly walked along the ridge and had a blast, to say the least. I had never hunted ruffed or spruce grouse. We did a lot of shooting and killed quite a few. After a couple of hours of grouse hunting, we headed back toward the house. As we walked across the field, I said to Bo, "Did you get a deer?" He responded, "No, Matt got one yesterday." I asked, "A good one?" "Decent buck," he replied.

We got back to the house and cleaned the grouse. I asked, "What do we owe you, that was great! Y'all going tomorrow?" He said, "You don't owe me anything. We'll probably go deer hunting tomorrow; if you want to go, be at the house about daylight." I said, "Sounds great."

David and I got in our truck and headed back to the motel. Time to start making notes of all that we had done. David also called Investigator Rogers and briefed him on what we had seen concerning the deer. He was happy and said that he was going to start putting together a team to execute a search warrant when we got through.

The following morning at daylight found us headed back down Bo's driveway. He invited us in and offered us coffee. I sat down with Jesse, who was reading a copy of the Idaho Fish and Game regulations. He told Matt, "I can't go deer hunting, I only have a small game license." Matt and Bo both responded, "You don't have to worry." Bo said, "I have a license and we'll only have one gun, so come on." Jesse thought about it a minute and said, "Y'all go ahead, I don't want to take that chance." Matt wasn't too happy, but I was, although I tried not to show it.

David was getting everything on tape. Matt didn't have much respect for game wardens, which was very evident, as he told about how many turkeys and deer he'd killed in Mississippi over the years and that his so-called buddy was a game warden. With that, he put himself on my hit list! I had just lost what little respect I had for him. Bo even showed a photo of Matt squatting by his Mississippi patrol car with several gobblers lying across the hood. Thankfully, Jesse didn't give in to their suggestive comments, saying, "Y'all go ahead, I'll just get a little rest and maybe go shoot some grouse."

We were all getting up and heading out. I actually wanted to shake his hand. I did say a little thank you to the Lord that Jesse was man enough to stand for what was right! David and I got in our vehicle and followed Bo and Matt through the curves of the mountain roads, stopping frequently to glass. As we rounded one curve, Bo's vehicle was on the side of the road and he was waving me up to him. I pulled alongside him, and he pointed to a fair white-tailed buck in a little draw about 150 yards from the road, saying, "Get him!" I pulled over, not liking what I was facing. Investigator Rogers had said, "Don't kill unless you must." I crawled to the edge of the road, hoping the deer would spook, but he didn't! I put the cross hairs just over his back and fired, missing. Bo gave me a look that I can still remember to this day. Then he said, "How did you miss that?," and he wasn't laughing. I knew we couldn't do that again. Fortunately, we didn't have to, as we didn't see anything worth shooting. After returning to Bo's house, David was able to sneak some photos of Matt's deer still hanging in the barn, untagged.

They talked of an elk Matt had killed a couple of years earlier, even showing us the photos, and mentioned several other deer. Bo also showed a photo Matt had sent to him from a car wreck he had worked, with what appeared to be several dead people in the vehicle, all covered with blood. On it he had written, "catfish bait."

Jesse came into the room where we were talking and told Matt that he needed to go to the airport. Something about a trial where he was going to have to testify. Bo said, "We can take you to the airport tomorrow, no problem." David and I shook Jesse's hand and told him to have a good trip, and we told Bo we would give him a call in a couple of days. Bo said, "Sounds good!"

David and I headed back to the motel. We gave Investigator Rogers a call from a payphone and let him know what we had for that day. He said he was ready to issue a search warrant on the deer and photographs we had seen. I called Agent Oliveri, and he started putting together a search warrant for Matt's residence in Mississippi. Not as much as we wanted, but we weren't paying the bill! David and I would not be involved with the takedown, but we were to call Bo and see what time he wanted us to meet him to go hunting. The following morning, David called Bo. He said, "Matt and I are going to take Jesse to airport today, be here at daylight tomorrow and we'll see if we can go find some elk." David said, "Will do."

The following day we just rode around in the mountains as if we were hunting. I drove as we discussed everything we had seen or heard and made notes. That evening we called Investigator Rogers, and he said they were going to serve the search warrant around 6:30 a.m. Agent Oliveri said he should have his warrant ready to serve at Matt's house in Mississippi that same day. The US attorney's office in Mississippi wanted Investigator Rogers to get copies of any photographs seized of Matt with big game kills in Idaho, so the search warrant team would be able to compare photographs with any mounted heads they might find at Matt's home. The snowball was rolling now!

David and I got up at daylight the next morning and loaded our gear, knowing that we were going to have to get out of the area pretty quickly once they served the search warrant. We drove up the mountain toward Bo's house and pulled off where we could just see the blacktop road that went to his home. Approximately 6:30 a.m., we saw a caravan of Idaho Fish and Game trucks headed toward Bo's home. I told David that we had just as well head back to Boise and wait on Investigator Rogers to call. We hit the highway and enjoyed the ride.

After lunch, Investigator Rogers called and told us they had arrested Matt and were going to charge Bo with aiding and abetting in state court, as well as possession of untagged game. The State of Idaho was going to charge Matt with hunting without a license, illegal possession of game, and possibly some other violations. They were transporting Matt at that time and would probably have a bond hearing that afternoon. He had confessed to shooting the deer; they also recovered numerous photos of deer and elk killed by Matt and other unknown individuals. Investigator Rogers said that he was waiting to hear from the feds on what they found with their search warrant.

Investigator Rogers came by our hotel room that afternoon and said that Matt was going to plead nolo contendere, which means he accepted conviction without pleading guilty to all state charges. He also said that the federal agents had seized some mule deer antlers as well as numerous photographs and other items. Matt would later be charged federally with Lacey Act violations—transporting illegally taken wildlife across state lines.

All persons charged except Bo pleaded guilty to all charges. David and I got one more trip back to Idaho several months later for Bo's trial. The trial only lasted a couple of hours, and he was found guilty.

I had to meet with the Mississippi Law Enforcement Internal Affairs Division concerning Matt. Although he was not fired, he was demoted in a disciplinary hearing. I had to return to their office one more time to let them know that a couple of law enforcement officers were looking for me. A federal agent contacted me and told me he had been stopped; the officer who'd pulled him over was asking questions about me. I trusted the Internal Affairs investigator I spoke with, and he said that he would look into it. I had my supervisor contact the game warden whom Matt had been running his mouth about; after speaking with him, we found out that Matt had asked him over to look at a video and see if he knew anyone, without telling him why. We didn't think about it, but Jesse had videotaped some of our grouse hunt. The video was later recovered by Internal Affairs and turned over to the federal agents. No one else was charged.

CHAPTER 12

THE BIG ONE: OPERATION COLD STORAGE

The first big covert investigation that the Mississippi Department of Wildlife, Fisheries, and Parks participated in was an idea of mine. I grew up trapping and knew the fur market well. I suggested making a route through Mississippi and Louisiana to buy fur (all legal). The MDWFP contacted the Louisiana Department of Wildlife and Fisheries' covert unit to discuss the potential joint investigation. The purpose of the fur route was not to illegally buy fur but to make contact with as many people as possible in areas where information had been obtained concerning the illegal sale of deer meat or game fish, as that would be the focus of the investigation.

Because the investigation would cross state lines, we asked the US Fish and Wildlife Service to be involved. They gladly joined the investigation. We worked with the US attorney on how any federal evidence would be handled and whom to contact in each state if the covert agents needed anything. The original plan was for the investigation to run for approximately eighteen months.

I was nervous as Ted, a special agent with the Louisiana Department of Wildlife and Fisheries, and I started our first route from Wilkinson County, Mississippi. We were working from a refrigerator truck with hidden cameras inside and out, as well as audio equipment, and had at least four stops planned in each state. About two weeks before the route began, we posted flyers with the approximate time we would be coming through and a phone number in Louisiana to call for information. Bill, the Louisiana agent, would take calls from individuals wanting to sell fur and relay the information to Ted and me. Our covert business was named Mid-South Fur Trading, and we had caps made with the business's name and phone number.

Our original plan was to be in Mississippi one day and then spend one day in Louisiana (twelve to fourteen hours per day). Ted and I would spend two days on the road trip, then day three logging evidence and other chores. We then transferred the legal items we'd purchased to refrigerator units and to other covert agents for sale. We would spend a week writing reports, logging and storing evidence, and so on, then hit the road and start again.

Our first day in Mississippi, I was somewhat on edge, as we had brought $6,000 in cash ($3,000 for Mississippi and $3,000 for Louisiana). By the third stop, I had already spent $2,800 of the money allocated for Mississippi. Things were going well, as we were making a pile of contacts. On our last stop in Mississippi, things got tense. Bill had already called us and said that he was getting numerous phone calls from folks mad that we had not shown up at our last stop in Vicksburg, Mississippi. We were running a little behind schedule, but our flyer stated between 7:00 and 8:00 p.m.; it was just 6:30 p.m. and we were en route. I told him, "Just tell them we're on our way!"

As we neared the old service station we were using as a pickup point, Ted said, "Oh my gosh, there must be twenty vehicles up there!" We rolled in and could tell that the mood might not be the best toward us from some of the looks we were getting.

As we exited the vehicle, the first subject who contacted us might have weighed 165 pounds, and was soaking wet and drunk as a boiled owl. He couldn't complete a sentence without including some vulgar m#@#$# f**)&##. To say the least, he was not happy and was stoking the fire with a couple of the other waiting, intoxicated individuals. It was good that we were able to get it all on video, as this individual, being the foul mouth that he was, couldn't shut up long enough to let us understand the problem! He was focused on telling us how his brother was "gonna beat our #%@%#" when he arrived. He reminded me of a Chihuahua dog that just wouldn't shut up. I finally heard from one of the other individuals that they had been there since 6:00 a.m.

While we were trying to explain that we weren't supposed to get there until between 7:00 and 8:00 p.m., the Chihuahua started up again as a truck pulled into the parking lot and much of a man unfolded from it. The Chihuahua said (with a few adjectives thrown in), "That's my brother! He's gonna straighten you two out!" As his brother (probably six foot four, 250 pounds) started toward us, Ted looked at me with a bit of concern in his eyes. I noticed that the fellow was carrying what appeared to be one of our flyers.

This gentleman was like E. F. Hutton; when he started talking, the rest of them, even the Chihuahua, listened. He stuck his hand out for a shake; I introduced myself and then Ted. I started to say something, but he turned to his wormy little brother and handed him the flyer. He then apologized to Ted and me before again turning to his brother and saying, "If you had looked at the flyer instead of running your mouth, you would see these guys are on time!" He further scolded the Chihuahua, who tucked his tail and walked into the crowd nursing his beer.

That stop was interesting, as we needed another couple of agents. As Ted and I were grading fur, weighing meat, and so on, we could hear all kinds of talk from the guys gathered around the truck. They discussed everything from headlighting deer, poaching rabbits, and illegally harvesting ducks to buying dope. It was definitely a target-rich environment!

The Chihuahua incident aside, our first day in Mississippi was a great success as we made lots of potential contacts. However, our major problem was that we had spent approximately $4,800 of the cash we had brought, all of Mississippi's money and $1,800 of Louisiana's money. We had a truckload of legal fur we needed to liquidate back into cash, so I called a fur buyer some distance away and asked if he would be interested.

Ted and I met with Jerry, a Mississippi agent, the following morning. We inventoried the fur and transferred it to Jerry's truck, and he headed to the fur buyer I had spoken to earlier. Jerry called back late that evening and said he had sold the fur and been paid $5,300, which gave us some breathing room. I told Jerry to take a photo of the check, then go to the bank, cash it, and bring the money to Louisiana. We met back up with Jerry later that evening and got the cash, as we were just about out.

We did not have quite the turnout in Louisiana that we had at a couple of the Mississippi stops, but we did make several good contacts. Things were looking good for Operation Cold Storage. We spent the third day at a hotel in Baton Rouge, inventorying tapes, going over notes of folks' names, digging up phone numbers, and putting them in a ledger for future reference.

You can really get to know someone spending twenty-four hours a day for three days plus with them. Ted was sharp as a tack, full of jokes, with quick comebacks to individuals' comments. He loved to read but was not a Christian. He told me that he was living with a girl who was religious. Once while we were traveling through Louisiana, we decided that we would stop at his house. He introduced me to Sheila, his girlfriend. She and Ted went in the kitchen to fix supper. As I was looking around in his den, I saw on a table what appeared to be a rock collection. As I was picking up the rocks and looking them over, Ted walked in and quickly said, looking back toward the kitchen, "Put those down—she worships those!" He didn't elaborate and I didn't ask any questions.

We worked well together, as we got along well but more so because we were as different as daylight and dark. I was the serious buyer and Ted was always joking, breaking the ice with some of the contacts who were standoffish. The cases were piling up, as we were getting in with some big-time poachers as well as frequently being offered narcotics, stolen guns, and other contraband. By the end of the first season, some major groups had been infiltrated, and the doors were continuously opening.

On the previous trip, an individual talked about introducing us to a subject who was moving a lot of meat (raccoon, deer, and crappie). We met the individual, and he asked us to follow him to a man's house to buy raccoon. He introduced us to Woodie, and we made a legal purchase of raccoon meat as a confidence buy, acting as if that was all we wanted. We had discovered that if we acted cautiously until we got to know someone, the subject illegally selling game would trust us, thus making things work smoothly when it came to an illegal transaction. Many times, we turned down the first illegal offer. It didn't take many purchases of raccoon before Woodie was selling us multiple deer and other illegal wildlife each trip. Everything was audio- and videotaped when possible, making things easier when it came time for a takedown.

After just a couple of months, the investigation was starting to pay off, as we'd made many illegal transactions involving more than twenty different individuals in both Mississippi and Louisiana. The MDWFP had to assign one agent just to resell all the legal fur that had been purchased. The Louisiana agency assigned an agent to keep the books on finances. The legal purchase amount on each trip was from $3,000 to $8,000. Trying to keep things separated was tough on us, and between fur-buying stops we would stop to make records of all expenditures.

From an administrative standpoint, this was great, as the investigation was paying for itself. Both of our supervisors, as well as the US attorney, were excited by the end of the first hunting season, due to the number of cases and potential cases.

By spring we were purchasing large quantities of illegal fish (primarily crappie) and being introduced to more targets. As we were making a purchase at one subject's home, he decided to show the agents his garden. He was very proud of his tomato plants, and, as the agents looked on, not really interested, they realized that he was actually showing off the way he grew marijuana! Between each tomato plant was a marijuana plant, another item to document as well as purchase. Each illegal transaction would generally lead to another.

One of the subjects was very open about his hatred for law enforcement as he showed agents his .45 caliber pistol he kept close by. He was a convicted felon in Louisiana and living in Mississippi. He knew that he would go to prison if he was convicted of any felony or caught in possession of a firearm. He made the comment that he would kill any officer who ever tried to put cuffs on him. We made several deer purchases from him over the coming months.

One thing a covert officer did was get to know people, and that information went into the file and would be brought up during the pre-takedown meetings later. Every time a new subject was predisposed to violate (i.e., showed knowledge that he was aware of laws he was talking about violating), a new file was opened with a background check for criminal history, driver's license photos, vehicles, home address, and the like. We had more than one hundred documented violations by the end of the first year. The plan was to focus more on the bigger players the second season, before we closed the investigation.

We set up a camper at a fishing camp for our base during the spring and summer on the Louisiana side of the Mississippi River just below Vidalia, Louisiana. Ted and I continued our route purchasing fish, both legal (catfish and buffalo) and illegal (game fish, primarily crappie or *sacalait* [French for crappie] as they are called in southern Louisiana), illegal turtles, and occasionally narcotics (marijuana and crack cocaine).

On one night, Ted and I were trying to locate an individual's home in a rural area south of Vidalia. We had been riding for about an hour when we decided that we would head back to the camp. When we got up on the Mississippi River levee, I noticed a vehicle brake light on a pull-off road we drove past. I kept watching the mirror and told Ted, "Bet that was a warden." We didn't want to get stopped.

Within a couple of minutes, I saw headlights moving swiftly in our direction. The vehicle, a truck, got right on our bumper; I could tell by a bar light across the cab, it was law enforcement for sure! The vehicle stayed up close, and I told Ted, "I wish he would go ahead and stop us!" I gave it the gas and left him; still no blue lights, but I could tell he was trying to keep up.

There was a road that went to a boat landing up ahead, and we decided to pull in to see if he was going to approach us; we did not want anyone knowing where our camp was. I turned into the boat ramp and just waited; the vehicle also turned in and slowly pulled past us. It was a constable, but he did not approach us. I pulled back up on the levee, and here he came again! We decided we would just pass the camp and go into town to grab some coffee.

As we could see lights from town up ahead of us, we could make out three vehicles at the city limits sign. They were local police, and the blue lights came on everywhere! We pulled over, and two that I could see in the mirror had weapons drawn. They were making a felony stop. We obeyed all their commands. They had me exit the vehicle first; with hands in the air, they made me walk backward to the patrol car, where I was cuffed and patted down. The same was done to Ted on the other side of our truck. I kept asking the officer who was doing all the talking why they were stopping us. All he responded with, as he came to me with my Smith & Wesson .38 caliber I had under the seat, was: "Is this stolen?" They were doing the same to Ted. He had a 9 mm in his door.

Thankfully, I guess they were so focused on finding drugs and our pistols that, while searching the vehicle, they didn't look at all the phone numbers in the back of a notebook I had lying on the dash. The front of the book had fish market names and phone numbers, as well as dates and times of pickups. The last several pages were phone numbers for the US attorney, federal wildlife agents, FBI agents, ATF agents, and game wardens from both states.

As nothing illegal was found in the truck and our guns came back clean, a couple of the officers eased to their cars, killed their blues, and headed into town. I shouldn't have, but as the constable who initiated the stop and the officer who had pushed me around a little were taking our cuffs off, I asked for their names and badge numbers. Not that I had plans to do anything, but I wanted them to think about it. Neither offered their name or an apology. There was an older officer who had been quiet until then; he brought our pistols and ammunition, and as he handed us our guns he said, "Sorry for the misunderstanding!" They got in their patrol cars and the constable into his truck, and all quickly pulled away.

We got in our truck and drove on into town. Ted said, "I ain't believing they did not notice your notebook and no one even looked in it. That was close!" We both laughed and joked about the incident that had taken place. It was a first. It's tough when covert officers cannot divulge their identity.

Thankfully, our undercover licenses came back clean with nothing they could question, and nothing came of it. If anything, it probably helped our cover with some along the river, as I'm sure there was coffee shop talk from the constable to some of the locals about the guys that bought fish getting stopped! No telling what may have been told, but it wasn't that we were law enforcement! We saw a couple of the officers later, but they never approached us again.

One interesting character Ted and I met was a heck of a commercial fisherman. He made his living off the fish he caught with nets along the Mississippi River and local lakes in Louisiana. His name was Chad, his entire family were commercial fishermen, and they had numerous run-ins with Louisiana game wardens as well as federal wildlife agents.

The store where we met Chad was a gathering place for many of the "river rats." They were suspicious of Ted and me in the beginning. We made several small, legal purchases, mainly just stopping by to slowly break the ice. Ted and I figured a couple of them out as they would hug us to pat us down for wires. They were smart! We didn't know at the time that this same group had been busted by a federal undercover sting several years earlier.

Another good crappie purchase that was a part of this operation. (Photo courtesy of the MDWFP.)

It took a couple of months of just hanging and not pushing anyone before the doors started opening. When they did, Chad took the lead as he seemed to be moving the most illegal fish (crappie). He was catching in Louisiana and selling in Mississippi and Louisiana, primarily peddling in small rural towns along the river. We started small, with purchases ranging from 50 to 150 pounds of dressed crappie. Our final purchase was 450 pounds of crappie (whole fish) for $800; he wanted $2 per pound, but he took the $800. Chad delivered and sold to us in Natchez, Mississippi, as we wanted to document Chad transporting across state lines. The fish were illegally caught, then transported across a state line and sold, and the value of $350 made it a federal felony under the Lacey Act.

We were ready to start winding things up with almost two years of undercover work and more than 150 subjects to be arrested in both states. Working closely with the US Fish and Wildlife Service, we thought it was time to start picking some off to see if they might want to help themselves before we concluded the investigation. We decided to start with Chad.

Chad had talked about all the individuals he was selling illegal fish to in Mississippi and Louisiana; so, we decided to see what he was doing and if he would take us along. I gave Chad a call and asked him to meet me at the Waffle House in Natchez to discuss some business. He agreed. We met the following morning for coffee and breakfast.

During our conversation, I told him I had someone I did business with who wanted to meet him. He said, "Great!" I said, "He just pulled in." We walked into the parking lot, where Federal Agent Kets was sitting in his truck. I tapped on the window, and Agent Kets got out of his truck. We shook hands, and I said, "Chad, this is Special Agent Kets with the US Fish and Wildlife Service." Chad laughed, shaking Agent Kets's hand, and looked at me, saying, "That ain't even funny!" I said, "He really is an agent for the feds and I'm an undercover agent for the state." I showed my badge briefly, as did Agent Kets, not wanting to make a scene.

Agent Kets shared a little of the documented violations against Chad and told him that if he wanted to work with us it might help him. We had already discussed this with the assistant US attorney assigned to the case. Chad was looking at thousands of dollars in fines, as well as substantial jail time.

Chad looked a little weak, as things were starting to sink in. He said that he wanted to talk, so we all walked back into the Waffle House and ordered coffee at a table in the corner, and Chad started sharing a lot of what he knew was going on illegally. We told him that we wanted him to take us with him on some of his runs so we could document the businesses that were purchasing illegal fish. He agreed. We had left Ted out, as we didn't want to expose him. We made it look like Ted was going to be arrested later, so if Chad did speak to anyone, Ted's cover would not be jeopardized.

Over the next couple of weeks, Chad held up his end of the deal, and we were able to document numerous businesses dealing in the illegal fish trade, both in Mississippi and Louisiana. When Chad was arrested, he was not charged with any felonies, just misdemeanors, and he was eventually sentenced to approximately $5,000 in fines and court costs, plus the loss of his privilege to hunt or fish in Mississippi and Louisiana for three years.

New Orleans Deer

Woodie, who had sold us a lot of deer meat in southern Mississippi as mentioned earlier in this chapter, was the best deer poacher I had ever come across. He was also a felon, having been convicted of armed robbery several years earlier. He stopped selling us deer and boastfully told us that he was selling to a bigger market. We had been dealing with Woodie for the past year; when he was killing deer, he was moving five to ten deer a week.

Several times I discreetly tried to get information about his buyers out of New Orleans. I think he thought I was trying to get into his market, so I backed off before he spooked and jeopardized the relationship. We tried surveillance for a while but were unable to discover anything.

Covert Sting

We were getting tired and ready to try to bring the covert part of the investigation to a close. It was time to try something different, if we were going to get the guys buying out of New Orleans. Ted, the US Fish and Wildlife Service agents, the MDWFP special operations supervisor, the assistant US attorney assigned to the case, and I met to set up a sting during the investigation. The purpose of the sting was to try and "flip" Woodie; hopefully, he would give up the buyers out of New Orleans.

I had earned Woodie's trust and believed that I could get him to take Ted and me headlighting for deer. If the sting worked according to plan, uniformed officers could make a stop and place all of us under arrest. Only one Mississippi game warden (the supervisor) was aware of what was going to take place. There would be two other state wardens thinking they were working a routine headlighting detail with federal agents because it would take place on federal property. During that type of sting, the fewer officers who knew, the less chance of a leak happening and possibly someone getting hurt.

I met with Woodie during the afternoon and told him that I was in a bind and needed some deer. I asked if I could go with him and get a few. Woodie seemed reluctant but said that he would. A time was set for us to pick him up that night. The plan was unfolding into the beginning of what would be a long night.

Ted and I picked up Woodie at 7:00 p.m. and headed for a national wildlife refuge along the Mississippi River below Natchez. During earlier contacts, Woodie had told me where and how he normally headlighted that area. There was a gravel road that went for miles through the refuge, with only one way in and out. The plan was for Ted to drop Woodie and me off and then pick us up at a certain point.

Federal agents and game wardens would be set up where the gravel road neared town. Ted would call one of the federal agents just before he picked us up. As Ted stopped the truck, Woodie and I hopped out of the vehicle into the darkness. As Ted proceeded down the gravel road, his taillights disappeared into the black night. Ted was supposed to pick us up two hours later at a location about a quarter mile from the drop-off.

Woodie and I eased down the edge of a field with no light except that provided by the stars. As our eyes focused to the darkness, Woodie showed why he would have been so hard to catch by normal means. Woodie was in good shape and walked quickly to put distance between us and the road.

The area we were hunting was very remote, and you could hear any vehicle for miles on that gravel road. The only sound other than the night was an occasional riverboat pushing its heavy load up the Mississippi. I loved it! Not only the rush of what I was doing, but it was a beautiful night to be out with no moon but stars as far as you could see.

Woodie was smart; he used a .22 caliber rifle. He told me to bring one also because it was quiet. He had a small coon hunter's headlight. Under Mississippi law, he would have appeared to be coon hunting, which was legal. He said that if we were to bump into a game warden, we would say we were coon hunting and the dogs had jumped a deer. This was a good cover story if we had no illegal game.

The area we were in was loaded with deer, and when Woodie turned his light on there were several sets of eyes glowing just inside the wood line. A large doe stood up with two fawns still lying under the brush; Woodie and I quietly crept to within fifty yards of the deer as they stared into the light. He slowly eased the gun to his shoulder, with the beam from the light staying fixed on the glowing eyes. With the crack of the .22 breaking the stillness of the night and echoing toward the river, one set of eyes disappeared; the other fawn quickly stood, and, with another crack of the .22, it disappeared, the doe running for safety into the darkness. Woodie cut off his light and slowly walked to where the deer had been. As our eyes got refocused to the darkness, I whispered, "Good shooting, you got both of them." "Shot twice," Woodie responded, as if, what did I expect?

While we were gutting the deer, I asked why he hadn't shot the big doe. Woodie responded, "Never shoot big ones, they are too much trouble to move." We sat and listened to see if any vehicle traffic could be heard on the gravel road. The silence was only broken by the owls cutting up in the distance. We each grabbed a deer and started toward the road.

After covering the deer near a tree, we went back to hunting. Woodie shot two more deer, and we followed the same procedure, leaving the guns with those deer near the road. We had to hustle to make it to the rendezvous location with Ted. Not long after we reached the location, Woodie said, "I hear a vehicle." We hid in the edge of the woods near the road until the vehicle passed and we could be sure it was Ted.

As the vehicle passed, I said, stepping into the road and flicking my light on and off a couple of times, "It's Ted." Ted stopped and killed the engine, allowing us time to listen for any other possible traffic. After just a few minutes—which seemed like an eternity—I flicked my light again and Ted opened the vehicle, allowing us to get in. Ted drove to each location where we had left the deer and guns near the road. We quickly loaded the deer into the truck and covered them. So far so good.

Things were about to get interesting. Everything was going as planned. Ted was driving; Woodie was seated in the middle. Even though we weren't talking

Documenting evidence is an extremely important part of the job. (Photo courtesy of the MDWFP.)

about it, Ted and I were both feeling a bit uneasy. As we had planned, the officer who knew what was happening would fall in behind our truck with lights off, then make the stop.

Adrenaline rushed when, out of nowhere, headlights appeared behind us. Then blue lights came on, and it got crazy inside the truck as Woodie frantically told me to open the door so he could jump out. I was trying to get Woodie's gun, in case he decided to do something really crazy. I said, "Give me your gun and I'll chunk it!" Woodie gave it to me, and I shoved it under the seat as Ted was stopping because two other vehicles were blocking the road with blue lights going! All the weapons we knew of were secure, except Woodie's knife.

As Ted slowly stopped the truck, lights (blue and headlights) came from everywhere. An officer said on the loudspeaker, "Driver, throw your keys out the window and let me see your hands, exit the vehicle, walk backward to the corner of the truck, get on your knees, cross your feet, and put your hands behind your head." This was repeated until, one by one, we were all handcuffed on our knees.

The game warden with knowledge of covert investigators appeared to search and handcuff Ted. The wardens who were unaware had their guns on Woodie and me, as was standard procedure on a felony stop. The officers (state and federal) separated Ted, Woodie, and me. I acted as though I was not going to cooperate and was placed in a vehicle with one of the unknowing officers, who was told to watch me.

As part of the plan, Ted appeared to be getting questioned while state and federal agents were reading Miranda rights and questioning Woodie. Ted and the state warden approached Woodie with Ted holding the handcuffs. The officers who did not know what was going on were surprised and excited when they found out that Ted was a covert officer. Woodie was even more surprised and knew he was in trouble. Ted joined in the questioning with federal agents as they made it appear that I was going to jail.

During the questioning, agents strengthened my cover as they asked about my business. Woodie would not give up any information on me. They reminded Woodie that he was looking at a minimum of four years in the federal penitentiary just for being in possession of a firearm. Woodie decided to cooperate and give up the people he had been selling deer to in New Orleans. I had been placed in one of the federal agents' vehicles like I was being transported to jail and was removed from the scene.

Woodie was taken to a hotel, where he was questioned and gave information concerning his New Orleans buyers; he told it all, in hopes that it would help him later. Agents strongly emphasized that if he changed his mind about cooperating, he would be looking at multiple felony charges. He agreed again to introduce agents to the buyers in New Orleans. He was taken to his home and told that he would be contacted by phone the following day with further instructions.

After much discussion and some arguing among the agents, I got my way and would be the one to contact Woodie. That next evening, Ted called Woodie and told him to meet him in the local Walmart parking lot. After a brief silence, Woodie said that he would be there.

I was with Ted in the parking lot when Woodie drove up. The cold-eyed, expressionless look on his face was one I had received many times before. Ted stayed in the vehicle as backup in case the meet went bad. I approached Woodie's vehicle on the driver's side. As I checked the vehicle for weapons and was assessing the contact, I noticed a Bible in Woodie's vehicle. I said, "I guess you know now that I'm an officer also?" Woodie answered with nothing more than a nod of his head.

The Word

I gave Ted a thumbs up and got in the vehicle with Woodie. As we continued our conversation, I mentioned the Bible on the console. I asked him, "Do you believe what's in that book?" His nod affirmed that he did, and I said, "If you do, we should not have any problems, because I believe it, too." We had a brief discussion about faith in Jesus. I shared with him that everybody made mistakes, and the greatest part was that through Jesus they can be forgiven. I could see a difference in Woodie as we had that discussion.

I got out of the vehicle and told Ted that Woodie and I were going to ride around for a bit, and I would get back with him later. Ted said, "You sure? Check in with me in a bit!" I said, "Will do." Woodie and I rode around during the evening and into the night, just being seen together. We also had a lot of discussion about God and life. Rather than the adversarial relationship I was expecting, Woodie seemed to befriend me. I had to be a little cautious, but I never felt that he was going to harm me.

Woodie held up his end of the deal by introducing me to the buyers out of New Orleans. We sold multiple deer on two occasions, once in Mississippi and once in Louisiana. During the second transaction, Ted was introduced to the subjects buying deer, to slowly move Woodie out of the picture. It worked perfectly, as the targeted individuals called me for their next and last purchase.

When the subjects from New Orleans placed an order for ten deer, plans for a large, multiagency "buy-bust" were set up. Only supervisors from the state and several federal agents met at the US attorney's office in Jackson for the first briefing. A second meeting involving all officers took place on the day of the buy-bust. I was surprised how amazed several of the state game wardens were when they heard how many deer had been sold and purchased during the previous eighteen months. After all officers and agents had been briefed on the backgrounds and seen photographs of the alleged targets, they were given specific orders on when and what to do to keep the situation safe.

The "buy" was supposed to take place at approximately 3:00 p.m., on the Mississippi side of the state line. Everyone stayed together where they met, with strict orders not to make any phone calls or radio transmissions until the bust took place for safety reasons. Numerous officers were disgruntled with the situation, as they didn't think things would happen as planned.

I received a phone call from the buyer confirming the deal. Officers and agents all got in their vehicles and went to their assigned locations to wait. Ted and I checked our video and audio equipment one more time before heading to the meeting place.

With the truck loaded with deer, Ted and I were excited and anxious, as that bust would start the closure of Operation Cold Storage. First, 3:00 p.m. came and went; then 4:00 p.m. came and went—still no buyer. One of the federal agents then drove up in an unmarked vehicle stating, "Doesn't look like they are going to show." I responded, "They'll show, I know these guys!" The federal agent seemed reluctant but said that he would tell everyone to hold tight. Ted and I both said, "They will show!" As he pulled away, Ted and I laughed about how many times we had sat for hours waiting on someone to show.

At 6:00 p.m., the federal agent contacted us and said that he was going to call it a no-show. I angrily responded, "They'll be here, but if you and the others want to leave, that's fine—Ted and I will handle it." The federal agent said that most of the officers were ready to call it. I again said, "They'll be here!" He paused before responding, "OK."

At that moment, my pager went off with an unfamiliar number. Ted broke radio silence (on a walkie-talkie) to let the federal agent know that we were going to return the call. We drove to a little service station, where I called the number from a payphone. It was the buyers; they had vehicle problems, were getting gas, and hoped to be at the meet in about thirty minutes. I said, "We'll be there."

Maybe not quite as planned, but it was going to happen. Ted contacted the federal agent in charge, forwarding the information. We were ready to get this one behind us. After returning to the location of the meet, we saw headlights coming down the dark, dusty road toward us. The pickup truck slowed, pulling up next to us, driver to driver. The subject was apologetic, and I, playing the character as all business, told him to back his truck to ours so they could get things unloaded.

Each deer was transferred to the buy vehicle and the money changed hands. Unknown to the four subjects who had come to purchase deer, federal agents located at the paper mill just down the road were listening to the entire conversation. The signal for the "cavalry" was when I recounted the money. That always seemed to be the longest wait.

As we were discussing another possible sale, the sound of approaching vehicles in the quietness seemingly threw things into slow motion. Headlights came from all directions, then blue lights, as the vehicles closed and abruptly stopped with officers jumping out, shouting that familiar phrase, "Hands up, law enforcement!"

Although Ted and I were facing the lights with our hands held just as high, we each had a sense of satisfaction as many long hours had gone toward apprehending those individuals. Handcuffed, leaning over the hood of the truck, Ted and I watched as the uniformed officers logged and photographed all the evidence, and the four guys from New Orleans were loaded and hauled to jail.

While the officers were basking in the glory of the big takedown, Ted and I slipped away, trying not to draw any attention. Going back to the hotel, we joked and laughed about the "glory" of an undercover agent—nothing more than a sense of satisfaction at a job well done. Time to do reports and log the evidence, video, and audiotapes of the transaction.

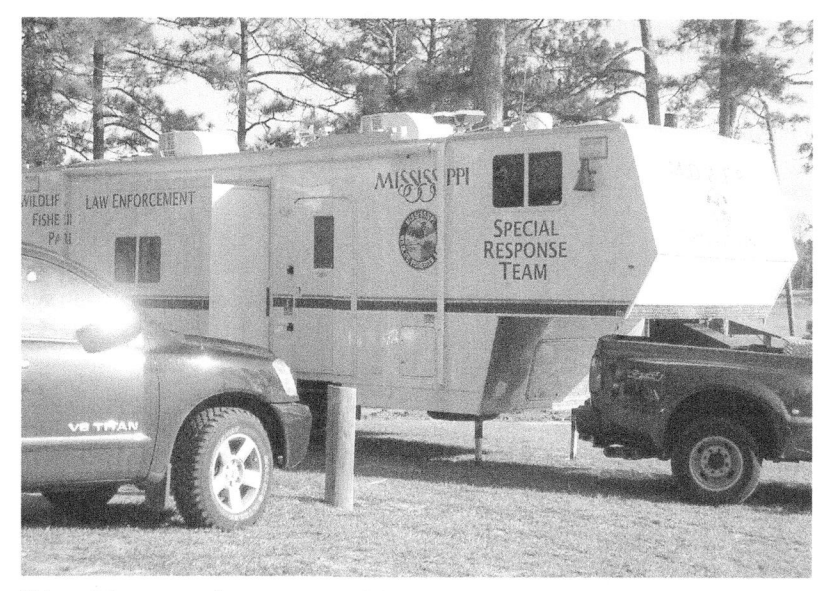

This mobile command center was used during multicounty operations. (Photo courtesy of the MDWFP.)

Roundup—Cold Storage

For the next several months, Ted and I worked on affidavits for warrants. Approximately 140 individuals in Mississippi and Louisiana would be charged with wildlife violations, including illegal take, possession, and sale thereof, and felony violations of the Lacey Act, as well as charging felons in possession of firearms and narcotics. It was the largest illegal wildlife bust ever in Mississippi.

Assistant US Attorney John Dowdy, US Fish and Wildlife Service agents from two states, ATF agents, US Marshals, and Mississippi and Louisiana wildlife law enforcement supervisors and covert officers met. We assessed each individual case file concerning charges to be filed for arrest warrants and the priority of the individual's arrest. If the subject gave agents a reason to be concerned about possible violent resistance, that person's file was pulled. We determined who would be apprehended and how to provide the safest execution of warrants for officers.

The state and federal agents put together teams of at least four persons for each warrant. During the several weeks it took to get warrants, we prepared files for each arrest team. Some teams would have numerous warrants to serve, calling on the local sheriff's department to transport subjects as they were taken into custody.

Each team was assembled by the warden supervisors who knew the wardens working in the counties, adding others with experience from across the state. The teams had no knowledge of what was going down. They were given a date to meet at a state park and to be prepared to stay overnight. That's all they knew, but they all suspected a major operation.

The team leaders met for a final briefing, led by John Dowdy. It included Federal Wildlife Agent Bobby Smith (federal charges pertaining to wildlife), ATF Agent Albert Faragway (seizure of weapons), US Marshal Bill Jones (handling subjects taken into custody), and Ted and me (to answer questions pertaining to each subject to be arrested).

The team had decided that the most violent of the subjects would be the first to be arrested, using a ruse to pull him out to the highway, in the open. Once that subject was in custody, officers in both states would get the green light to execute arrests, notifying their central command upon each completed arrest.

Team leaders advised their individual teams to make any personal calls before they were briefed, and only emergency calls would be allowed after briefing. It was vital that nothing leak out about the plans for the following day, as it involved five counties in Mississippi, four parishes in Louisiana, and approximately one hundred arrests to be made in one sweep. I didn't sleep much that night, as I knew the following morning would bring closure to almost two years of a covert investigation. And I was ready!

I had one last meeting with the US Marshals along Interstate 59, and we decided on the signal to arrest: I would remove my cap and place it on the hood of the truck. The plan was this: I would call the subject to try to get him away from his home by telling him that I was broken down on the highway just up the road from his house.

As the predawn light was starting to break through the trees along I-59, it was finally time. I drove off alone, but there were "eyes on" as the marshals were just below the intersection where the subject should approach. I made the call, waking the subject and asking if he might come help me, because my truck had broken down. Almost makes one feel bad to do that to someone, even if he is a criminal. He thought enough of me to get out of bed and come to assist me on the road.

The phone call worked, and the subject said that he would be there in a minute. I radioed the marshals, telling them it was about to happen. I had my hazard flashers on and the hood on my truck up. I pulled a plug wire loose from the vehicle so the engine wouldn't crank, sat back in the vehicle, and adjusted the mirror to watch for the subject's vehicle. Those could be some of the longest waits; time always seemed to go into slow motion on such occasions.

As the target's vehicle approached, my adrenaline started to pick up. As he approached my vehicle, I got out, shaking his hand and leading him around to the engine with the hood blocking his view of the oncoming vehicles. I removed my cap and placed it on the cab of the truck. As I heard the gravel crunching, I slowly eased to the other side of the engine, putting a little distance between myself and the target. With the sound of car doors opening, I heard the shout, "US Marshals, get your hands up!"

As we both were getting handcuffed, the target was bent over looking at me with confusion. We were escorted to separate vehicles, where my handcuffs were removed. At that very moment, all the different teams across Mississippi and Louisiana started making arrests. The last of the more than one hundred arrests were made approximately nine hours later. I was both physically and mentally exhausted as I made my way home.

It was somewhat humorous when I watched the evening news and saw that several of the subjects who had been arrested that day were wearing the caps we had given out with our (covert) company's name on them. They never knew what the bull's-eye on the back of the cap with the arrow sticking in it meant. As the case had progressed, those caps had been given to any subject who had committed a violation of some sort.

Woodie in Court

Woodie was brought before a federal judge after working out a plea agreement with the assistant US attorney. Due to his previous felony conviction (armed robbery), he was charged as a felon in possession of a firearm, but no other charges documented during the investigation were filed. After the attorneys got through with the normal legal "chitchat," the judge sentenced him to four years in federal prison. Although I didn't show it, it hurt; Woodie and I had actually become friends. As he was being escorted away by US Marshals, he got my attention. The marshals allowed him to stop and speak to me in the hall. It was brief. I put my arm around his shoulder; I still remember the tears in his eyes as he was escorted away. God be with him! One of the federal wildlife agents, looking confused, asked me what was going on. Not knowing how to explain, I didn't comment. I never saw Woodie again, although I still wonder whatever became of him.

Work Interrupted?

During this long, covert operation, my wife and I were getting more active in our local church. It made things hard on me, as I had started teaching a Sunday School class. Still working undercover and teaching Sunday School didn't seem

Even undercover mission work was a part of the job.

to fit together. Although some of my students knew what I actually did, seldom would anyone ask. I had long hair, normally pulled back, with a heavy beard.

God had a plan for me even though I was still working undercover. Betty (my wife) had gotten involved with the church's mission committee and was feeling led to go overseas. She asked me what I thought about her going to Africa, with my first response being: "That's not for us, and I'm too busy with Operation Cold Storage." She kept praying and asked me to pray about it.

I mentioned my wife wanting to go on the missionary trip to my supervisor and the chief of law enforcement during a meeting at the office. I felt like I needed to protect her (as though God wasn't already going to do that). They were both Christian men and told me to go on the trip. They said that the takedown could wait until I returned. "Do what?" I thought.

About this same time, the 9/11 attack took place and the world seemed to be in lockdown. But still, the missionary team was planning to go as soon as the airports were opened back up.

God was truly working on me, with the anger of much of the country toward the Muslim community, and now I was going to a Muslim country to witness. It got confusing, to say the least.

I started praying, and the next thing I knew, Betty and I along with several others from our church and our youngest son were boarding a jet, headed to somewhere in Africa!! Be careful what you pray for!

My second trip to Africa.

Upon our arrival in North Africa as "undercover missionaries," God showed us that He was in control as we approached a checkpoint. I had very dark olive skin, long dark hair, and a dark heavy beard. I fit in with the area of Africa we were at, as most of the Muslim men there had that same look. However, Betty has fair skin and blonde hair, so she stuck out. Our group was prayer walking, visiting orphanages, and smuggling Bibles into an overwhelmingly Muslim country. There were a couple of missionaries with us who had done this before, and they said that we might get searched and the Bibles seized at the checkpoint. They laughed about it, saying that either way, the Bibles would get distributed, because the military persons who seized them would then sell them.

As we approached the gate, we decided to pray that all would go well before walking up to the checkpoint. We had to pray silently because of local laws. After praying, we continued to the checkpoint where there were numerous military personnel armed with AK-47s. I almost laughed and cried at the same time as we got closer to the gate, knowing that the armed individuals were not seeing our little group of missionaries. They acted as if they were facing a "tank"! Their eyes were fixed as our group walked through the checkpoint. Not one of our bags got searched, nor were there any issues. The guards at the checkpoint just backed up, letting us pass through. We didn't know what they saw or heard, but we knew that God was there with us. When God is in the midst, miracles are taking place.

God was opening my eyes as well! I did not quite understand what "prayer walking" was or what to do! The only thing I could do was pray, and oh what God was going to show me. To see a believer in Christ who would lose everything, possibly even their life, for Christ's glory made me see life from a whole different perspective.

On a visit to an orphanage, Betty and I along with the rest of the team arrived at feeding time. It only took place once a day there! Children from infants to twelve or thirteen years of age were there at this time. It was so sad to have to hold back the larger boys like animals, as they were so hungry, fighting just to eat! Diapers were changed only once per day due to lack of diapers and people to help. We had brought diapers to take to the orphanage, so it was perfect timing—God's timing!

After spending a couple of weeks in that part of the world, one realizes how truly blessed the citizens of the United States are. Running water, electricity, and many other daily blessings are taken for granted at home. Upon our returning home, I looked at the world quite differently, even my work.

CHAPTER 13

TURTLES GOING TO CHINA!

Investigating the turtle market was interesting. We had been looking into several of the licensed turtle farms across the state, and everything appeared to be in order. It is a controlled market, as no new permits are being issued for turtle farms. The turtle farms that had been established before a certain date were "grandfathered in" and are the only turtle farms operating in Mississippi.

The farms primarily raise red-eared sliders. In the spring when the sliders would lay their eggs, farmers dig up the eggs and place them in incubators. The survival rate is typically over 90 percent in a hatchery, as compared to less than 25 percent in the wild. Farmers can also harvest eggs from the wild, but they are supposed to release a certain percentage of them. There is much room for violation, if no one knows exactly what is harvested and what is released.

The turtle biologist who normally worked with the farms, Bryan, believed that something was going on with one of the larger farms in the Mississippi Delta, near Clarksdale. He said that he couldn't put his finger on it, but they were up to something. Bryan is a sharp biologist, and, if he said that something was up, I believed him. We started snooping around, watching what was going on, and we didn't come up with much, other than that someone from Louisiana was coming and going a good bit. After running his tag and following up on him, we learned that the frequent visitor, Robert Jones, owned a turtle farm in Louisiana.

I contacted the owner/permit holder of the Clarksdale farm, Joseph Hampton, and told him that I was wanting to get into the business. He was quick to tell me I couldn't, saying, "You have to be grandfathered in, and the state isn't issuing any new permits." I told him I had gotten a permit to trap turtles out of farm ponds and was catching a bunch, but said, "I'm supposed to release them." He kind of laughed and said, "Stop by one day and we can talk about a place you could release them."

The following week, I showed up with a truckload of sliders in bags. When he came out to the truck, he said, "Get those out of here, I'll meet you down the road!" I drove down the road and pulled over under a big tree to wait. He showed up and flagged for me to follow. I followed him down the road a couple of miles before we turned into a large field. After we went through some woods on the other side of the field, I saw a fenced-off pond, with tin around the bottom. It was definitely a turtle pond. He didn't have this one on his permit list. By law, he was supposed to allow the state access to all of his turtle-farming records. He paid me a shabby price for the turtles, but it gave us enough evidence to get a search warrant.

Because the turtles were being shipped out of state, I contacted US Fish and Wildlife Service Special Agent Robert Oliveri to see if he might be interested in assisting me with the case. He said, "Definitely!" We worked with the US attorney's office to obtain a search warrant. Agent Oliveri, Bryan (the turtle biologist), and I met with John Dowdy, the assistant US attorney, to discuss the case and to present evidence of illegal activities and what we believed might be going on. At the time, we thought that Mr. Hampton was just collecting more than he was reporting.

We were issued a search warrant by a federal magistrate after John Dowdy presented the case. We executed the warrant on Mr. Hampton's home, office, computers, vehicles, and all outbuildings. We had a team of top-notch wardens and federal agents, as well as Bryan, to execute the warrant, but we had no idea how big of an operation it was! We found documents and bank records everywhere, in shoeboxes, garbage bags in the closet, and the fax machine. The phone didn't stop ringing the entire time we were there. The faxes were orders from businesses in China.

When we left his place, we had a truck with a camper full of paper documents and a Suburban, two computers, photographs, and video footage of the entire operation, including the ponds and incubators. Agent Oliveri interviewed Mr. Hampton, but he cut it short when he said he wanted a lawyer before he would continue to talk. Agent Oliveri gave him a business card and said, "Have your lawyer contact me."

The following day we started going through all the documents, mostly just separating bank records and shipping documents; one name that kept popping up was the Backwoods Turtle Farm in Louisiana. We needed an accountant to help with all those numbers! We found Robert Jones's name and number throughout. It was time to give him a call. During our brief conversation with him on the phone, he denied knowing anything about the Backwoods Turtle

Turtles Going to China!

Special Operations Agents Dustin Blount, Glen Jackson, and Gary Smith removing an alligator from a turtle net while investigating illegal turtle marketing. It was never a dull day! (Photo courtesy of the MDWFP.)

Farm. We decided it was time for someone to have a sit-down with Mr. Jones, as the bank statements we found had his name on them. Agent Oliveri contacted Bill Mellor, a US Fish and Wildlife Service agent in Louisiana, and emailed him what we had found, as well as some questions to ask Mr. Jones.

According to the State of Louisiana's records, there was no Backwoods Turtle Farm. We continued with our investigation of the paperwork. The bank records showed significant deposits from Hampton and Jones, as well as electronic deposits from several businesses in China. We needed a numbers guy and someone who could help figure all of this out on the computer. I have never been so tired of looking at documents in my life.

We finally put together that they were laundering the illegal sale of hatchlings as the Backwoods Turtle Farm to cover their excess profit from illegal sales to China. They had done a good job. That little bank account held over $100,000. We could show that they were shipping extra turtles under that bogus business name.

When Agent Oliveri and I met with Mr. Jones, Mr. Hampton, and their attorneys, things didn't start off very well. Agent Oliveri said, "We'll just have the Internal Revenue Service look into our investigation." Then they started asking for a plea agreement real quickly! They each pled guilty to federal Lacey Act charges and paid $10,000 in fines, as well as having their businesses each being placed on a five-year probation. If they were caught during that probationary period with any illegal turtles, or documents not in order, everything would be brought back up and the plea agreements would be voided. I thought they got off lightly, considering the amount of money they were making off the illegal trade, but we did our part.

CHAPTER 14

DEER, DOPE, AND BEER: OPERATION TRIANGLE

Operation Triangle began after we received information from a game warden in Lauderdale County, Mississippi, concerning individuals headlighting and selling deer along the Mississippi and Alabama state line, covering three counties. He had the names of the individuals and a lot of good intel concerning their activities. The warden also had an informant who was willing to work with us. We decided to first try on our own without involving someone we did not know. The fewer people who knew what was going on, the less chance of a leak.

We decided that one undercover agent would try to contact the poachers as a poacher himself. We leased some property and set up a camper near where the poachers were supposedly hunting, hoping that casual contact might open the door to get to know them. Undercover Agent Jerry Gibson spent several weeks at the camp and finally started bumping into the targeted individuals at the local stores and bars.

Before long, they were stopping by Jerry's camper to show off the deer they had killed. Some general conversations about hunting, and boasting by Jerry, triggered the same type of bragging from one of the poachers, Marty. He asked Jerry if he'd been killing anything. Jerry responded, "Been killing a few." Marty, about half stoned at the time, responded, "Where you putting your deer?" Jerry said, "I have a fellow that comes by and picks them up. All I have to do is gut them."

That got their curiosity going. They did not ask much more, but Jerry could tell they were ready for one of our ruses. I told Jerry we would get a couple of deer and wait until they came by for a visit. The ruse would make it appear that I was buying deer from Jerry. After many years of covert work, I had found that it was a lot easier to introduce someone to a buyer than to try to buy yourself.

I was driving a small Chevy S-10 with a camper shell that was wired with covert video cameras. I pulled up to Jerry's camper, and the waiting game began. Finally, after several hours of peeking out the window of the camper, Jerry said, "There they come." The ruse began. I turned on the cameras in the truck and started covering the two deer carcasses with a tarp. Jerry was helping me, when two gruff-looking fellows stepped from their truck. They could see the deer as we were closing the tailgate and camper window. One of them said, "Y'all had some luck?" I did not say anything, but Jerry replied, "A little."

Jerry introduced Marty and Frank to me. While shaking each of their hands, I told Jerry that I needed to go. I walked not out of their view, but to the side of my truck. Pulling out my wallet and removing a large of amount cash, I called Jerry to the side of the truck away from the targeted subjects. I counted out $150 and whispered to Jerry, but loud enough that they could hear, "They alright?" He spoke out, "Man, they're cool." I responded, "Be careful, I don't need any trouble." Shaking Jerry's hand, I told him to give me a call when he got some more. I got into my truck to leave and, as I pulled away, I told the targets, "Nice to meet you."

Jerry gave me a call a couple of hours later, acknowledging that the ruse had worked. The targeted individuals were asking how much he was getting for deer from the fellow in the truck. In wildlife covert investigations, you want to establish that your targets are predisposed to sell. During conversation with the targets, before Jerry told what he was receiving, he asked if they sold deer and their price. Once they admitted they had been selling, and their price, the door was open to further investigation. All conversations were being recorded.

During the next few days, Jerry continued to talk with the targets to build their confidence, telling them that I (the buyer) wouldn't buy from them because I didn't know them. Jerry set up a buy for Friday of the following week. Jerry told the targets, if they killed anything, to bring it by Friday morning before 10:00 a.m. and he would sell for them. He explained that I wasn't comfortable buying from them, and he would get their money. He made it clear that I wouldn't purchase skinned, processed meat or anything that had been gut shot. He said I was very particular about the meat. This enabled us to make better evidence photos with whole deer.

Approximately 10:00 a.m. that Friday morning, Marty and Frank brought two gutted deer to Jerry that they claimed they had killed the night prior. Jerry told them to put the deer in his truck and cover them with the tarp lying there. He gave me a call on his cell phone while sitting in the camp with them: "Hey boss, got you a couple, you still coming by?" I responded, "Be there in about thirty minutes." Just prior to pulling into the camp, I pulled over, turning on recording equipment and prefacing the tapes.

As I pulled up, Jerry, Marty, and Frank exited the camper, making their way to Jerry's truck. I backed my truck up to the rear of Jerry's as they were letting the tailgate down. I got out, and we all shook hands and made brief small talk as I asked Jerry, "You got a couple?" Laughing, he said, "I told you I would have some! You want us to load them up?" As I looked into the open cavity of one of the two dead does in Jerry's truck, I said, "Load 'em up." Marty and Frank each grabbed a deer and started loading as I paid Jerry. They were in hook, line, and sinker!

After I got the deer covered up, we sat around the camp, and the stories started to roll out. The more beer the targets drank, the more it seemed to loosen their jaws, as they kept telling how many deer they had killed by headlighting and other illegal activity. Another individual drove up to the camp and joined the group. After they introduced John, he went back to his truck and returned with a joint lit up. As he took a long drag and passed it to one of the other fellows, it was evident we had another target. As the joint was offered to me, I quickly told them, laughing, "I don't smoke that crap!" I was holding a beer and acting as though I was drinking it. They just laughed and continued to pass it around, telling their boastful stories of how they had evaded the game wardens over the years.

During the next couple of weeks, I made several more buys of deer they had killed. Even though I paid Jerry, he would turn and hand one of the targets the money, all being video and audio recorded. They offered to take us deer hunting one night. I acted cautious and refused, telling them I didn't need any trouble with the law. I did mention to the guy who had the marijuana that my wife liked that crap, and could he check with his "man" about getting me a little? He laughed, saying, "How much you want?" I said that she was pretty particular and didn't want junk, but I would be back the next week and to have me a "dime bag." He said, "No problem."

The next week, Jerry and I had planned to meet on Thursday, and he had advised the targets that if they had any deer, I would be coming through. Jerry also told John (the one with the dope) that I would be there. He said he would have it. Things were expanding, as we had made multiple deer buys (eight deer) and were setting up a narcotics purchase.

As I pulled up to Jerry's camper on Thursday just before dark, I saw two vehicles other than Jerry's. While pulling in, I turned on my video and audio recorders sewn into my vest, giving the date and time before I got out of the vehicle. Jerry went into the camper, and while the men loaded the deer into my truck, I went ahead and paid Frank, as that was our third purchase. After paying for the deer, the other individual (John) walked up asking if I still wanted some weed; I said, "Sure, if it's good." He said with a chuckle, "I don't sell nothing but good stuff." He then pulled an approximately one-ounce bag of weed from his pocket and said, "That'll be a hundred dollars." I pulled out a roll of cash and counted out $100, all being recorded.

Jerry walked out of the camper and I told him, "I thought you were going to have more meat than this." He said he hadn't had a chance to kill anything. One of the targets quickly spoke up, asking, "How many you want?" I said, looking at Jerry, that I needed a couple more, insinuating that Jerry had let me down. The target said, "Well let's go get 'em." I acted hesitant, and Jerry said, "Come on, we can take my truck." Still being hesitant, I agreed. All had been preplanned, as we wanted to document them headlighting deer as well. We made sure we were in Jerry's truck so we were in control of the vehicle and everything was being recorded, as his truck had hidden cameras in the cab. I had notified the game warden who had initiated the investigation that we may go headlighting that night and what type of vehicle we would be in, in case he got a complaint. He was not to tell anyone. The only reason he knew was in case something went wrong; he would know where and for whom to start looking, if I did not contact him the following day.

Marty grabbed a cooler full of beer out of the back of their truck while Frank grabbed his .30-06 out of the cab, and we piled into Jerry's extended-cab, white Dodge truck. Marty and I got in the back seat, with Jerry and Frank with the .30-06 up front. We left camp around 7:00 p.m.

Frank was telling Jerry where to go. I was trying to pay attention to the road signs (Jerry or I would call out the name of roads during conversation so it would be recorded on tape), but after about four turns and lacking any signs, I had no idea where we were headed. I could tell we were heading east of Meridian, Mississippi. We made several turns and were on gravel roads to nowhere!

Frank was telling Jerry, "Slow down, there is a good field around the next curve." As we rounded the curve, the headlights of the truck covered a small field where a large doe and two yearlings stood frozen in the headlights. Jerry stopped the truck and, no sooner had the crunch of the wheels in the gravel stopped, the loud *kaboom* of the .30-06 broke the stillness of the night. The large doe crumpled to the ground; the two yearlings were still frozen as the second round fired, dropping one of them. The second yearling broke for the wood line but stopped before entering the cover of the trees. It dropped as the third shot echoed from Frank's .30-06. With three deer down in less than a minute, I thought, "He's definitely done this before."

Frank, Marty, and I took off into the field to drag the deer back to the truck. It was a small cornfield, but recent rains made it tough getting the big doe back to the truck. I grabbed one the yearlings and headed to the truck. Marty and Frank dragged the large doe and slung her into the bed. Then Frank took off at a dead run to the other side of the field to retrieve the other yearling. The rush of adrenaline was going, and we needed to get out of there, as we didn't need to get caught!

That Dodge was slinging gravel to get us away from the area. As Frank bragged about his shooting, Marty started asking about the weed I had purchased earlier, wanting to "roll one." I told him, "That was for my wife!" After we got out of the area, we pulled over and Marty grabbed four beers from the cooler, each of us popping a top to act as though we were celebrating our accomplishment. A little farther down the road, I told Jerry to pull over, saying, "I need to take a leak." Jerry knew what I was doing, as we had done this before. I stepped away from the vehicle and, while relieving myself, sat my beer down on the ground out of sight. I was able to turn the beer over, allowing it to drain. Jerry was doing the same on his side of the truck. We could appear to be drinking just holding an empty can. We did not need any alcohol in our system.

As we approached another field, Frank said, "Stop, stop, there's one!" From the back seat I could see a house not far from the field. I told Frank, "Don't shoot, there's a light on in that house." He kind of giggled and squeezed one off; as fire rolled out of the barrel and the thunder from the .30-06 rifle echoed across the little bean field, the deer dropped. As taillights popped on from a vehicle at the house across the field, I shouted to Jerry, "Go! Go! They're coming!" Frank barely made it back in the truck, almost getting run over as Jerry was slinging gravel trying to get past the driveway where a vehicle was backing up at a high rate of speed. Jerry was probably doing sixty miles per hour as we passed the driveway, and then the unknown individual was on our bumper. As chaos erupted in the truck, everybody was telling Jerry how to drive.

Thank God, the road was very dusty, and whoever was chasing us either hit the ditch or gave up; I'm sure he called the law. As we rounded a curve with a deer standing in an old graveyard, Frank said, "Stop! Stop!" "No!" I shouted, but Jerry already had the vehicle stopped and Frank fired, the yearling doe falling to her death as the bullet hit. Frank and Marty jumped out, grabbed the deer, and threw it into the back of the pickup. In doing so, they slung blood all over the silver toolbox, the side of the white truck, and the back window! They jumped back into the truck laughing, saying, "Find us another one."

I said, "You stupid idiots! Don't you know the law is already looking for us?" Give me the gun and get out of here, Jerry! Take me to my truck." Frank reluctantly gave me the gun, and I unloaded it and put it under the seat. Jerry said, "Which way?" Not having a clue where we were, I said, "Just go west 'til you hit a blacktop road!" Frank and Marty were asking to stop so they could grab some beer at a store. As we reached a road, not having a clue where we were, Jerry turned right. Seeing a road sign, Jerry said, "Oh crap, we're in Alabama!"

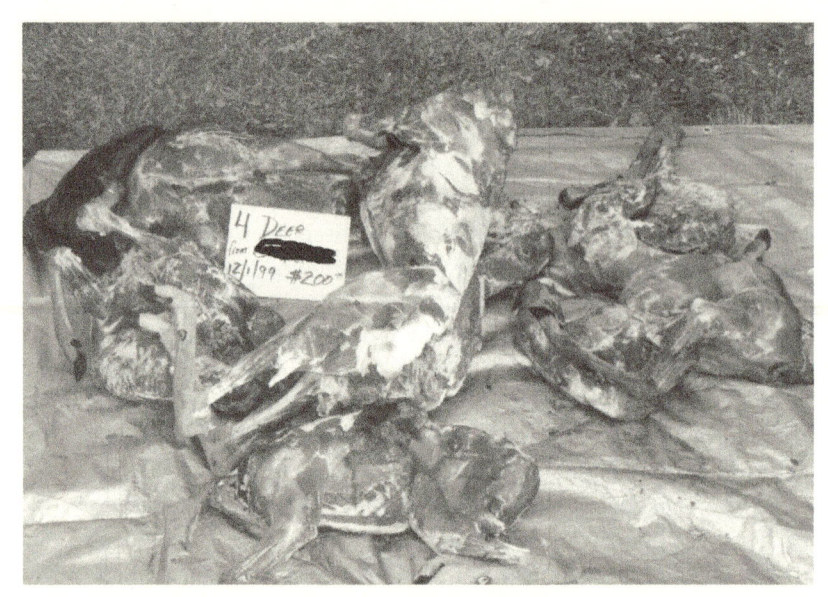

I frequently purchased deer. (Photo courtesy of the MDWFP.)

Somehow, as we were running from that vehicle, we had crossed from Mississippi into Alabama. Not good! To make things worse, as we topped a hill, there were blue lights everywhere! Frank started throwing out beer cans, Marty was trying to get me to throw out the dope, and Jerry was freaking out! As Jerry slowly approached the roadblock, a fight broke out between the officers and a drunk from the vehicle in front of us, leaving just one young trooper at the checkpoint.

I was saying a prayer: "Lord, please don't let us get arrested in Alabama!" Jerry handed the officer his driver's license, and the officer stepped to the back of the truck with four dead deer lying in the bed, blood all over the side of truck as well as on the toolbox and back glass! That vehicle looked like it had been sprayed with blood. Thankfully, the young state trooper was wanting to get over to help his partners wrestling with the drunk on the side of the road. He quickly handed Jerry his driver's license, saying, "Y'all be careful." As Jerry slowly pulled away, I watched with amazement out the back glass, wondering how we made it through that one. Then I remembered, I had asked God.

Frank and Marty said, "Let's go back and get the deer we left." I said, "Y'all can, but not with me in the truck." Jerry was looking in the mirror at me when I said, "Get us back across the state line." Jerry just nodded. Arriving back at Jerry's camp, we threw the deer into my truck. I paid Frank $200 for the deer and asked Jerry to go with me, that I needed him to help me with something.

They asked, if they got the other deer, would I be around to buy it? I told them no, that I had to make another pickup.

As Jerry and I were pulling away, the horizon was starting to get orange to the east, and I looked at my watch, then at Jerry with a little laugh, saying, "It's been a long night." Jerry said that he hadn't thought we would ever make it through that roadblock. I praised his driving. He laughed and said he didn't know how we didn't wreck! Now the work began of logging in the evidence (dope, deer, video/audio tapes, shell casings, etc.) and making reports. The fun stuff!

Marty and Frank, along with numerous other individuals Jerry and I had been working covertly with for approximately nine months along the Mississippi/Alabama state line, were later arrested. We documented numerous misdemeanor and felony charges including headlighting, sale of deer, and multiple narcotics (XTC, marijuana, and methamphetamine) sales.

CHAPTER 15

OPERATION AST: LACEY ACT VIOLATIONS

Special Agent Robert Oliveri of the US Fish and Wildlife Service called me and said that someone was trying to sell alligator snapping turtles on the internet in northern Mississippi. At that time, I was not familiar with the internet and didn't get too excited about what Agent Oliveri was telling me. He gave me a phone contact of the individual supposedly offering the turtles for sale. I told him I would try to contact the individual.

I came up with a story and gave the person a call. The individual said that he had already sold to a fellow in Arkansas. I told him that I was a contractor building a restaurant for someone who wanted an alligator snapping turtle in a large aquarium. He said that the person he'd sold to was a turtle farmer in Arkansas and he might sell. He gave me the individual's number, and I gave him a call. His name was Mr. Hamilton.

The subject in Arkansas said that he already had the turtle sold. "How big was it?" I asked. He said it was approximately 125 pounds. "Man, that was just what I needed!" I exclaimed. Then I gave him the same story about the restaurant and asked, "What would he take for the turtle?" He said, "I have some smaller ones I'll sell." I said again, "My client really wants a big one." He said to give him a call the following day, as he wanted to think about it, and I agreed.

When I called the following morning, he said, "I'll sell him for $2,500, no less." I said, "I don't know about that." He said, "Take it or leave it, I can ship him tomorrow after I get him tagged." I said, "Let me check with my client and see if he is willing to pay that much. I'll get back with you in just a bit." I quickly added, "You're not setting me up, are you? A friend of mine told me to be careful buying those things, that it was illegal in Mississippi." He just laughed and said, "I want cash and I'm not going to tell anyone, just don't say you bought it!" I told him, "I'll call you back."

I contacted Agent Oliveri and told him what I had; he said, "Try and set up a buy." I called the turtle dealer back and told him, "My client is willing to pay that amount, if it is over 100 pounds." Then, playing dumb to try to win his confidence, I asked, "What do I need to put him in?" I told him I would be coming from Jackson, Mississippi, and to give me directions to his place in Arkansas. He said it would take close to four hours from Jackson, and he then gave me his address. I asked if Friday afternoon would be okay, and he said that would work, as the Arkansas Game and Fish Commission biologist was coming Thursday evening or Friday morning to tag him. He then said, "Give me a call when you leave Jackson." I confirmed, "$2,500?" He said, laughing, "Cash!" I agreed, saying, "See you Friday."

Agent Oliveri set up a takedown team for Friday afternoon with federal agents in Arkansas and the Arkansas Game and Fish Commission, who had no knowledge of this individual engaging in the illegal wildlife trade. Agent Oliveri also had the federal agent in Arkansas get a search warrant for the subject's place and notify the assistant US attorney who would be handling the case, as it would be a felony case under the Lacey Act, which made it a federal offense if illegally sold wildlife valued at more than $350 crossed a state line.

We all met on Friday morning at a state park in Arkansas, about an hour from the subject's residence. Agent Oliveri and I briefed everyone on the covert details of the case and how we would handle the buy-bust and search warrant. I called the subject during our briefing to confirm our deal, telling him, "I should be there around 1:30 or 2:00 p.m." He said, "I'll have him ready for you. See you when you get here."

At 12:30 p.m., I headed to his place with the others not far behind. All but Agent Oliveri and another federal agent would stop at their waiting points, not too far away but out of sight, until they received the signal to do the takedown. Agent Oliveri had a surveillance point where he would be able to watch the transaction. When the deal was done (money and turtle exchanged), I would take my hat off and place it on my truck. That was my physical signal in case my transmitter/wire failed. We always tried to have a secondary plan in case technology failed (as it had before!).

All went well, as Mr. Hamilton was eager to sell that big turtle. After he showed me the beast of a turtle (125 pounds), I counted out the $2,500 and paid him. After paying, I took my cap off, laying it on the cab of my truck. We then loaded the turtle into my truck, after putting it in a large, wet burlap bag. He said that the biologist had tagged it the day before with a chip, then laughed. He had told the biologist it was a brood turtle he had raised in captivity.

Special Operations Agents Gary Smith, Dustin Blount, Glen Jackson, and me (left to right) with a large alligator snapping turtle we had purchased. (Photo courtesy of the MDWFP.)

As we were standing at the back of my truck, Agent Oliveri and the others involved in the bust came rolling up and placed Mr. Hamilton under arrest. After the search warrant was served and Mr. Hamilton was interviewed, he admitted that he had purchased the turtle, as well as three other alligator snapping turtles (all illegal transactions), from the subject in Mississippi where the case originated. The other turtles were seized; they were 80 to 110 pounds. His computer and numerous records, as well as the money I had paid him, were all seized and handled by the Arkansas Game and Fish Commission and the federal wildlife agents in Arkansas.

Those seized turtles were used to set up busts of purchasers in numerous cases throughout Arkansas, Louisiana, and Mississippi that summer, before they were released in a federal wildlife refuge that borders the Mississippi River. They became celebrities and got to see more highway than most turtles.

Mr. Hamilton pled guilty to federal Lacey Act charges and was fined $5,000. He also lost his turtle ranching license in the State of Arkansas for three years. Operation AST, for "alligator snapping turtle," was a success.

CHAPTER 16

SWEET VICTORY: THE CARROLLTON ZOO

After the takedown in Arkansas with Operation AST and the seizure of the four large alligator snapping turtles, we decided that before we released the turtles, we would use them to see if we could get in with a different illegal market. We had information that a zoo in Carrollton, Mississippi, was dealing in illegal wildlife, and those turtles might be a way to open the door.

The zoo had caught my attention the year before, so I stopped and looked around, posing as someone just looking at the animals. I documented several native species that were in captivity, as well as very poor conditions of some of the exotic animals, but never contacted the owner. Selling live wildlife was a very different element, as we could only make one sale and then had to bust the individual. We could not allow the animals to leave our custody. It was illegal to sell or purchase alligator snapping turtles in Mississippi and Arkansas. It was also a federal violation of the Lacey Act to illegally buy anything from another state.

Working with Special Agent Robert Oliveri of the US Fish and Wildlife Service, and the assistant US attorney, John Dowdy, we put together a plan. Before we could make any type of case, I had to make sure that the owner of the zoo knew the turtles were illegal, to establish predisposition. Agent Oliveri and I put together a team that would execute a search warrant at the zoo if everything came together with the sale.

I contacted the owner of the Carrollton Zoo, Mr. Davis, by phone. I told him that I was a commercial fisherman, had caught some big alligator snapping turtles in Arkansas, and was told that he might be able to help me move them. His first response was, "How big are they?" I said, "Eighty to one hundred ten pounds." He said, "That's some good ones, how much you want for them?" I said, "I can't sell them in Arkansas, it's illegal and I don't need any trouble with the law!" He laughed and said, "You don't have anything to worry about here, how much you want for them?"

I acted a little reluctant and said, "I got to bring them across the state line and if I get caught with them, the feds will put me under the jail! How much will you give me?" He said, "Five hundred for all of them!" I laughed and said, "I'm not taking that big a risk for five hundred. I'll bring them to you for seven fifty." We haggled on the price and he said, "I'll go to six fifty, but no more." I said, "I'll get back with you tomorrow and let you know." He said, "I want them, bring them. I'll pay cash! You need to come see my zoo; we can probably do more business. I have a big area with lots of different turtles, but none that big." I said, "I'll call you tomorrow."

I called Agent Oliveri, and we discussed how we would handle the takedown. We would need the state's herpetologist and another biologist to help identify any odd species during the execution of the search warrant. He said, "Set up the deal for next Thursday morning around eleven o'clock, and that should give us plenty of time." I laughed, saying, "You know these things never go as planned." We had checked all zoo licenses in the state as well as captive wildlife permits, and Mr. Davis had none. Agent Oliveri found out that, at one time, he had a zoo in the state of Louisiana but had his permit revoked after being caught with illegal animals there. He had been operating in a rural area of Mississippi for approximately ten years.

I called Mr. Davis that evening and asked if he was still interested in those turtles. He said, "Sure, $650?" I said, "I'll go with that just to get rid of them, but I don't want any trouble!" He came back with, "I told you, you don't have to worry about anything here!" I said, "It'll take me 'til about 10:30 or 11:00 to get there if I leave early Thursday, OK?" He said, "Sounds good; see you then."

I was headed to the Carrollton Zoo on Thursday morning, after a quick briefing with the takedown and search teams at a state park not far from the zoo. Just before I reached the zoo, I pulled over on the side of the road, turning on the video equipment, body wire, and recorder that I was wearing.

I pulled up to the zoo, and Mr. Davis came out of a little house next to the entrance. The zoo was behind a wooden fence that hid any animals from the road, but there were signs along the road advertising the place. I introduced myself to Mr. Davis, and he immediately asked, "Let me see the turtles." We walked to the back of my truck, which got us in front of the hidden video camera in the toolbox. I dropped the tailgate and pulled the tarp off the turtles. He said, "Those are some big ones!" I acted nervous, shut the tailgate, and covered them back up. I said, "Don't want anyone to drive up and see these in my truck, I don't need any trouble!" He laughed, "I told you, you don't have anything to worry about here!"

I said, "They would put me under the jail, bringing these things from Arkansas." I had Arkansas plates on my truck. I was giving him every opportunity to change his mind, making it very clear that what we were about to do was illegal. He said, "I'll go get your money. Pull around and back up to the big gate by the house." I got into the truck and did as he asked. I could see one of the unmarked vehicles slowly driving by with state and federal agents. They were getting a little impatient.

Mr. Davis returned, and when he handed me the money, I counted it out loud, so Agent Oliveri and the others knew that the deal was done. That's when things always seemed to go in slow motion, waiting on the arrest team. As I was putting the money in my pocket, he was opening the gate. We each grabbed a turtle and started into the fenced area. I could hear gravel crunching as several vehicles pulled up to my truck. The parking area held five law enforcement vehicles, two US Fish and Wildlife Service unmarked trucks, and three MDWFP trucks.

They handcuffed us both and told us that we were being arrested for the illegal sale of alligator snapping turtles. After we were Mirandized, they separated us, placing me in one of the state vehicles. Mr. Davis was extremely aggravated and was swearing as well as making threatening remarks. He was transported to the local jail to be questioned.

During the takedown, Mr. Davis's wife came out, and she was very close to joining him as she started making threatening statements and swearing at the agents and wardens. One of the wardens finally got her calmed down and explained to her that they were about to issue a search warrant on the house and the zoo. She said, "I'm calling our lawyer!" The warden told her that she was going to sit down or she was going to jail, too! She sat in a chair on the front porch smoking a cigarette. She was tough!

As the zoo was searched, Agent Oliveri and one of the wardens questioned Mrs. Davis about their zoo. She stated that they had all their permits and that it was a city zoo. She was unable to show any proof of it being a city-owned zoo. The search of the zoo uncovered several native wildlife species (snakes, birds, raccoons, coyotes, foxes, alligators, and turtles) that were illegal to have in captivity. We photographed each animal in its cage and documented them for evidence. There were also exotic species that required special permits to hold, such as lions and tigers. They seemed to be in poor health, and they appeared malnourished.

During the search, the agents seized numerous documents from the house as well as several young, dead tiger cubs that were in a freezer. We had information from another case that the Davises had been selling tiger cubs, but investigators had been unable to prove it at the time. The search and seizure of the illegal animals went on into the night. Mr. Davis had bonded out and returned home before we were through. We almost had to place him back under arrest due to his threatening remarks about wanting to kill agents. We had two agents sit with him and his wife until we were through.

The information obtained in the search warrant gave us numerous state charges as well as federal Lacey Act violations. The Davises pleaded not guilty on all the state charges. The first time the case went to court, the judge dropped all the charges. The local prosecutor had refused to meet with me on several occasions, saying, "Y'all do not have a case, it's a city zoo." I could tell that this was not going to be easy; we were fighting the local court, and they were behind Mr. Davis all the way. That was the system sometimes in rural areas; we were the bad guys! I refiled the charges, and another judge, who had recently retired, was assigned the case.

We had another day in court. The wardens and I all showed up for court on the date shown on the subpoenas. After a brief time sitting in the lobby of the courthouse, one of the clerks got my attention as she motioned for me to step into another room. She whispered to me, "They are planning on dismissing the charges."

The prosecutor for the county came in and walked right past us as if we weren't even there! I was furious! The judge called us into the courtroom, and I have never seen such a circus in all my years of law enforcement. The prosecutor was playing with the judge's gavel and talking with the defense attorneys like he was on their side! After the judge read the charges against Mr. Davis, the defense attorneys and the prosecutor approached the bench. The defense had a document they handed the judge, with a copy presented to the prosecutor.

The judge read the document and asked the prosecutor what he thought. The document was a typed statement on city letterhead, and not even signed, that said the zoo was owned by the city. The prosecutor agreed that Mr. Davis could not be charged, as he was not the owner. The judge said that all charges were to be dismissed and the animals were to be returned to the zoo.

I asked the judge if I could see the document, which was totally out of order in court, but this was a joke! I approached the bench and told the judge after reviewing the document that the animals could not be returned according to state law, reading to him the state statute regarding captive wildlife. The judge asked for a recess to talk with the attorneys.

The defense attorneys were hot, to say the least. They started telling the judge that the state couldn't do that and that I could not approach the bench during court. The judge was about as confused as the rest of the courtroom. So I added to the chaos by saying if they dropped the charges against Mr. Davis, then I would refile the charges against the city! The defense attorneys and the prosecutor laughed, saying, "You are out of order and you can't do that!" The judge ordered a recess and said we would meet at 1:00 p.m. for his final decision.

We had about an hour and a half before the circus resumed. I told Warden Toby to come with me: "We are going to visit the mayor!" Toby said, "Are you sure?" I said, "We are going to see if this little town is ready for what we are going to give them." I was mad! We went into the mayor's office. His door was open, and I could see him looking at me as I approached his secretary's desk asking to see him. The mayor overheard and told her to send us in. I introduced myself and Warden Toby. He was very polite. He could probably tell from my demeanor that I was upset. I have a hard time hiding my anger sometimes.

I asked the mayor if he was aware of the charges recently filed against Mr. Davis. He said, "Yes, I've heard about it." I then told him that Mr. Davis's defense attorneys said the zoo was a city zoo. I then asked, "Is that zoo owned and maintained by the city? Does the city receive any finances from the zoo?" Before he said anything, I told him, "We have served a search warrant on Mr. Davis's home and business and have not found any correspondences with the city concerning the zoo, its operation, or any financial records of transactions between them. The zoo was documented purchasing illegal wildlife and holding illegal animals in captivity."

The mayor was quiet for a moment. He then said, "The city does not actually own the zoo, it is just called the Carrollton Zoo. They have always called it that since it's been here." I said, "Was the city aware of the illegal activities of Mr. Davis, and would the city want to take the responsibility of the animals and the way he has been operating the zoo?" He said, "We were unaware of his activities and take no responsibility for what he has been doing." I then asked if he would write a letter stating what he had just told me on city letterhead and sign it. He agreed. The mayor then wrote a letter stating that the City of Carrollton did not own the zoo, nor was it aware of any of the activities there. It was just called the Carrollton Zoo due to its location. He then had his secretary type it up and asked me to read it before he signed it. After I read what she had typed, I handed it to the mayor, who signed it. I thanked the mayor and shook his hand, as Warden Toby and I left his office headed back to the courthouse for round two.

I was confident now that the judge would not drop the charges. As we were walking toward the courthouse with the letter in hand, I noticed on the letterhead the city attorneys' names. They were the two who were defending Mr. Davis. Oh, what a can of worms we were fixing to get into. I loved having an ace in the hole!

When we got back into the courtroom, the judge slapped his gavel, stating that court would reconvene in the case of *State v. Mr. Davis*. Before he said anything else, I asked if I could approach the bench; again, totally out of order, but what the heck, this court had been out of order since the beginning! Not waiting on an answer, I walked toward the bench with the letter in hand and said, "Your honor, you may want to look at this before you go any further." I handed him the letter from the mayor; I had highlighted the two attorneys' names.

The two defense attorneys were going ballistic with, "We object!" They and the prosecutor were threatening to have me charged. They followed me to the judge, and, after he read the letter, he handed it to the prosecutor, who then handed it to the defense attorneys. Oh, I wish I had a picture of the looks on their faces as they read what the mayor had written contradicting their statements, plus the fact that I had highlighted their names. I commented to the judge that the letter would be held as evidence, and, if they wanted, I would be glad to make them a copy.

I asked Warden Toby, making sure everyone could hear, "You did get up with that reporter with Channel 4 news, didn't you?" He responded, "He said he was on his way!" It was just a ruse, but it sure sped things up. I knew that those attorneys wouldn't want all of this on the evening news.

It got really quiet in the courtroom, and if looks could kill, the two defense attorneys, as well as the prosecutor, would have killed me numerous times! I just smiled and, though I shouldn't have done it, as one of the defense attorneys looked back at me, I winked at him and whispered, "Gotcha!" The court seemed to deflate, as they didn't know what to do. The attorneys asked if they could consult with their client. The judge agreed and set another court date.

Finally, we were able to get a conviction, as the new defense attorney entered a plea of guilty on a couple of the charges against Mr. Davis. For some reason, the original defense attorneys no longer were representing Mr. Davis. I wondered if they still had a job with the city.

I was glad the case was finally over, or so I thought! Mr. Davis undoubtedly got every attorney he could find to sue the state and each one of the agents involved, and we were tied up in civil court for the next five years. Sadly, I had to fight with the state's attorney not to settle. Finally, after Mr. Davis had exhausted all of his means, it was over and his illegal operation was completely closed down. This case was a good lesson in fighting a corrupt system. Thankfully, the law finally prevailed, but it was a tough road to victory!

CHAPTER 17

CRAPPIE AND WHITETAILS ALONG THE MISSISSIPPI RIVER: OPERATION DELTA

After Operation AST, the Arkansas Game and Fish Commission asked if the Mississippi Department of Wildlife, Fisheries, and Parks would do a joint investigation with them, like we did with Operation Cold Storage. We decided we would try, but with the fur market falling, it would be harder to establish the same cover. After much discussion, we decided that we would try two separate covers. One used two covert agents (one Arkansas agent and one Mississippi agent) with a covert commercial fish buying route; the other used two agents who would sell fish bait and tackle, establishing a similar route starting in the Greenville area of Mississippi and traveling north along the Mississippi River through Friars Point to Tunica. On the Arkansas side of the Mississippi River, we would work the river north from Lake Village to West Helena and as far north as Jonesboro. We had two campers set up at Lake Village as well as one near Friars Point.

We started that spring, with Charles (in Arkansas) and me managing the fish route and Jerry (in Mississippi) and Don (also in Arkansas) driving the fish bait and tackle route. I had established numerous contacts during the previous several years in these areas and had made some small illegal purchases of crappie and paddlefish roe. Charles had also been working along the Mississippi River, so that made it easier to get started. We were pulling a flatbed trailer with two freezers hooked to a small generator. We also had hidden video recorders in the vehicles as well as in the wall of one of the freezers.

We purchased quite a few catfish from numerous commercial fishermen. We would then take them to another location and resell the legal fish, trying to keep our cash flow up. We started picking up a few crappie from several of the commercial fishermen as the spring turned into summer. I was the buyer, and Charles worked for me.

This was Charles's first big case to work. As we spent many days together, we became good friends. It was evident that he was a Christian, but he went to a Pentecostal church and I went to a Baptist church; that brought up some good discussion for a long day in the truck. We had Bible drills some nights when we all met at the camp. It was fun, as we would argue about different theological beliefs, not that any of us were qualified. But I felt that, because we all believed that Jesus was our Lord and Savior, He was using this as a way for us to dig deeper into His Word.

On one evening, all the agents met at the campers in Lake Village and had a cookout. Charles had brought some venison and was frying up some steaks. Jerry, who was quite a big fellow, was eating the steaks as fast as Charles could cook them. Charles was getting a bit frustrated. I told Jerry to go to our camper and get some more cooking oil, trying to give Charles time to get us some steaks cooked.

I had picked up a large bobcat on the road that day and skinned it after Charles and I got to camp that evening. When Jerry walked away, I went and cut the backstraps out of the cat, which was hanging in the tree behind the camper. By the time Jerry got back, Charles was browning up some of the bobcat steaks. We didn't tell Jerry!

Charles and I watched with anticipation as he was placing the crisp, brown cat steaks on the tray and Jerry dug in. He gobbled one up and, as he reached for another, asked Charles, "What did you put on this; it's better than the other!" Charles and I looked at each other not saying anything; we each grabbed a piece for ourselves. It was delicious! When we told Jerry, he turned kind of green; we all laughed, but needless to say, all of the cat got eaten.

One unique part of Operation Delta started during the middle of the summer. Things were slow due to extreme heat; fishing was slow as well. I had picked up a large rat snake crossing the road and had it in the toolbox of the truck. I told Charles that it would be a good way to start a conversation, as people are always amazed with snakes.

We had pulled up at a boat landing on one of the oxbows along the Mississippi River, where some pretty rough locals were sitting around drinking beer. Charles and I got out, sat on the tailgate, and popped a top just to blend in. We sat just talking, then I got the big snake out of the toolbox and started playing with it; within minutes, several of the group that was there had walked over to admire the snake. Didn't take long and the whole crew was around our truck. They even lit up a joint and offered us some. They burned a couple of joints and then smoked a little crack through the evening. A small thunderstorm had come up, so we all moved under an old leaning shed to get out of the rain. Charles had gotten his recorder turned on, thankfully, as their jaws were flapping—they were primarily talking about sources to purchase narcotics. There was also some talk of selling deer.

The ringleader of the bunch, a man named Joe, was bothered by a big red wasp that kept flying close to his face; he was getting annoyed and swung at it. He slapped one of the old support beams, and an old rusted nail stuck completely through his hand! Good thing he was high; it took Charles and I both to pull his hand off that old nail. We were now Joe's buddies. A snake and a stoned idiot would open a big can of worms over the next couple of months! Joe gave us his phone number and said, "If y'all need anything just call me and I can fix you up. I mean it. Anything!" Joe didn't know during his evening of talking that he had given the names of several of his drug suppliers; one was supposedly selling deer, also.

After we'd made several small purchases of weed from Joe, he began to talk about a fellow who killed lots of deer and sold the meat. Charles and I were very interested in this fellow and asked Joe to introduce us. It took a little time, as the guy was cautious and we didn't have any information on him. When we finally met him (Clint), we knew we had a winner after running the tag on his truck. Clint was a felon convicted for the sale of narcotics and numerous other charges in the past, including some involving wildlife. He was very cautious at first, but after the ice was broken and we had a couple of small purchases under our belt (wildlife and marijuana), Clint started to open up.

He invited us to his residence, which was in a very rural area along the Mississippi River in Arkansas, and oh, did he open up! He offered to sell us numerous guns, still in the box. He had a roomful of guns still in their boxes. He elaborated on how he and Joe had been stealing guns and fishing equipment from different Walmarts in the area. He said that they would go in, look at a firearm, and place it in their buggy along with other items. One of their wives would be pushing the buggy. The other wife would drive a vehicle around the store behind the lawn and garden area, where the store grounds were fenced in. They would act as if they were putting something large in the buggy, placing numerous items (box with gun, etc.) on the ground. While moving around, they would shove the items they were stealing under the fence to the vehicle on the outside, making sure the vehicle was blocking any surveillance footage of the theft. Undoubtedly, they were pretty good, judging from all the guns they had, as well as rods and reels.

We purchased several of the cheaper guns to establish ourselves, so we would be able to come back later. When we left, we went to the prosecutor's

Crappie were purchased during Operation Delta. (Photo courtesy of the MDWFP.)

office in Little Rock and shared what we had on Clint and Joe. Things got kind of humorous, as the Arkansas State Police had a special task force set up trying to catch Clint. They had pictures of Charles and me going to and coming from his place. We'd been making numerous other purchases of deer and crappie both in Arkansas and Mississippi. The police didn't know who we were and had put us down as potential targets. I guess our cover was working really well. When it came time to take Clint down, we decided to do a buy-bust, with Charles and I getting arrested as well. Clint was a big fella and didn't want to be handcuffed. It was humorous watching him and four game wardens rolling around on the ground!

Night at the Bar

During Operation Delta, through some of our contacts along the Mississippi River, we had found a little bar that cooked steaks on Wednesday night. Several of the individuals from whom we had been purchasing illegal game and fish as well as narcotics frequented the bar. On one particular night, Charles had two agents, and I had two agents, meet us for dinner. I had already shown Charles how I would purchase a beer and, after a few minutes, go to the restroom and pour it out to fill the bottle with water, so I could later kill it and order another to appear as if I were knocking them out with the rest of the folks. This worked well for me over the years.

The thing about this night that I wanted to share was how our men watched Charles and me. As we all went in and pulled a couple of tables together, the waitress came around to start taking orders (she was the only waitress at the bar). I ordered a Coke, Charles ordered a Coke, and each of our men, seeing that we had not ordered a beer or other alcoholic beverage, followed suit. Being that we were in a small bar where everyone could see us, it was almost humorous that a table full of covert law enforcement officers (as rough as we looked) all were drinking Coke or Sprite.

The waitress never questioned us, nor any of the individuals who would come over and speak to us. I even got up and sang karaoke with one of the fellas that we had made purchases from, "Mammas Don't Let Your Babies Grow Up to Be Cowboys." It was hilarious, and it showed me that God was watching over us; we even asked for a blessing when our steaks were served. Several of the guys made jokes over the fact that no one acted suspicious because we were the only folks not drinking alcohol. I believe that God made them blind to what we were doing and protected us.

Sammy

Prior to Operation Delta, I had made a contact with an old commercial fisherman who ran a fish market in Clarksdale, Mississippi. I would stop by when in the area and discuss fish prices and the like. Over about a year's time of hanging out with Sammy, we had become pretty good buddies. I made several small purchases from him and sold him legal fish that I had purchased in a different area. He was beginning to take me in, as we started running nets together. During Operation Delta, I continued to use Sammy, as we could leave boats and trailers at his home, and he was introducing us to other fishermen along the Mississippi River, not only in Mississippi but in Arkansas and Tennessee as well.

On one occasion, Sammy asked if I wanted to go with him to catch some buffalo, as he was running low on buffalo inventory at the market. I said, "Sure." We hooked up his boat full of nets and headed out. As we pulled up to a public boat ramp, there were numerous vehicles with trailers in the parking lot. I could see a large sign posting the lake regulations. One of the regulations that stood out was, "No commercial fishing." I asked Sammy about it. With a little laugh, he said, "We not gonna be here long." After unhooking, he climbed in the boat and said, "Back me in." I agreed, backed him in, parked the truck and trailer, then ran and jumped in the boat. He sped across the lake, where numerous boats could be seen fishing; most of them undoubtedly knew Sammy, as they would wave as we went by. I thought to myself, this is going to be interesting, setting illegal nets in broad daylight where several folks can see us! One thing I knew was that this was not Sammy's first time!

We sped across the lake to the upper end. As Sammy slowed the boat to just a little more than an idle, he pointed to an anchor tied to the net and told me, "Just slip that over the side." I did as I was told, and Sammy just kept going as the net slid over the side of the boat. We had just about closed off a shallow cove with netting when we reached the end of the net. I then, at his direction, flipped the other anchor over the side. The net was set.

Sammy had not stopped the boat as he turned into the cove heading toward the shallower water. As we eased into the shallow water, you could see the wake from large buffalo heading in all directions. Sammy had a rusty, old, single-barreled shotgun that he was loading; the barrel was swollen near the end and even had a split in it. He slid the gun over the side of the boat with one hand, the other still on the motor, as we were still easing along. He then said, with a big grin, "Watch this."

When he pulled the trigger with the barrel in the water, fish headed toward the net, and you could see the floats, barely visible, bobbing as the fish hit the net. He reloaded, discharged the gun one more time, and said, "Let's go load up and get out of here!" We pulled the net with a load of fish in it—and I mean a load, primarily buffalo, and a few carp. We were loaded and headed back to the landing all in less than an hour from launching the boat! This was definitely not his first time. I had never seen a shotgun used to run fish, but it definitely worked! We probably had five hundred pounds of fish and didn't even seem to attract any attention. A few minutes at the landing and we were gone. Sammy was a sharp "old river rat," and through his introductions, we were making numerous cases (paddlefish roe and crappie).

On one occasion, Sammy and I went out to shoot coons from a boat (which is illegal). After we launched the boat, we motored out to the center of an old lake, where Sammy told me to kill the motor, as there were a couple of camps that still had lights on. He said, "We'll wait 'til everybody's asleep before we start huntin'." As we sat in the middle of the lake with no light, the stars in the night were overwhelming! It was a beautiful night; there were so many stars you could almost reach out and touch them.

As we sat quietly in the boat just gazing at the beauty of the night, I broke the silence, saying, "The stars are amazing tonight." Sammy responded, "Do you believe in God?" I thought to myself, this is awkward, as I am trying to document this fella's illegal activities and he is asking about God. I responded,

"Yes, I believe this is all His creation for us to enjoy." He didn't respond for a few minutes, but then said, "Makes you wonder," as I could see him looking into the vastness of the night with stars as far as you could see. He didn't say anything, nor did I, until he said, "Let's go kill some coons."

We motored around the edges close to the shoreline, killing several coons as well as a few rabbits. We saw several deer that would have been easy targets, but Sammy had enough wits about him not to kill deer. I asked, "You don't ever kill deer?" He said, "No, they'll get your license if you get caught shooting deer. They'll just write you a ticket if you're shooting rabbits and coons." Thought to myself, "That's smart."

During the close of Operation Delta, no charges were filed against Sammy (he had never sold us anything illegal), but several of the people he had introduced us to were arrested. I didn't call him, as I figured he knew that I was an undercover game warden. A couple of months passed, and Sammy called, "Where you been?" I said, "Been busy." He kind of laughed and said, "When you going to be back up this way?" I was not sure if he was joking or what, so I just told him that I would holler next time I was up that way. He said, "Stop by, I want to talk with you." About a month later, I called Sammy as I wasn't too far away. He said, "Come by and I'll make some coffee!" I said, "I'm headed your way, be there in about thirty minutes." He seemed almost excited. I wasn't sure what to expect.

Sammy greeted me at the door as if nothing were wrong. He said, "Where you been, haven't seen you in a while. Want some coffee?" I said, "Sure." As his wife entered the room, he poured up coffee and we all sat down at the kitchen table. He said, "Been wanting to tell you something, but didn't want to do it over the phone." I thought, "Oh, crap, this is going to be about all his buddies getting arrested!" My mind was covering all kinds of things until he finally spoke. He said, "Guess what?" I didn't know how to respond and just hesitated, waiting on who knows what. His wife said, "Tell him!" Sammy said, "Our son is going to the seminary!" Nothing about folks getting arrested, not a word! I said, "Congratulations!" He excitedly told about his son's decision. I was overwhelmed with the joy I saw in Sammy and his wife and definitely saw God's hand in what had taken place. Although I'd only spoken with his son a few times over the years, it was evident that Sammy had influenced his son's decision. When I left Sammy and his wife, both said goodbye and invited me to stop by anytime. That was the last time I ever saw Sammy. I do believe one day I'll see him again in heaven, as I do believe he is a brother in Christ.

CHAPTER 18

DUCK MERCENARY

One particular contact I made at a wildlife expo in Mississippi opened up a big federal waterfowl investigation. I bumped into a fella who was offering guided duck hunts in Arkansas. He asked (as I was admiring his photo album), "Do you like duck hunting?" I said, "Not really, but I love killing them!" He responded with a little laugh and said, "We could get along!" I started making comments about extreme numbers of ducks. I laughed and introduced myself, inquiring about prices for hunts and locations. He said that he had a guide service in Arkansas, and I told him I would get back with him. We seemed to click, and I felt that he may have been crossing the line after looking at his photo album.

I passed the information on to US Fish and Wildlife Service Special Agent Robert Oliveri in Mississippi and Charles of the Arkansas Game and Fish Commission. We decided to take it a little further and book a hunt. I called Toby, the owner of the guide service, and asked about the upcoming teal season. We decided to go on a teal hunt in eastern Arkansas in the fall to see just what kind of operation he was running.

Charles and I stayed at a small hotel and spent considerable time with Toby and a couple of his guides, as well as other hunters. The hunt didn't go well, as there were very few teal, but Toby did show that he was willing to violate the law when he started directing us to shoot shovelers, as the season was not yet open for shovelers.

After a poor hunt only killing a few teal and listening to Toby's foul mouth for a couple of days, Toby, who is from Louisiana, invited Charles and me to go on a hunt with him in North Dakota. He said they slaughtered the ducks up there and, from the stories we had heard, it sounded interesting. After checking, we found out that it was illegal for a nonresident to guide hunts in

North Dakota. The US Fish and Wildlife Service said that they would cover the cost for Charles and me to go. We booked a hunt for the beginning of the duck season in North Dakota.

Neither Charles nor I had ever been to North Dakota, and we were looking forward to the trip. We flew into the state and rented a four-wheel-drive Ford Explorer. We tried to rent a truck, but to no avail. The Explorer was new and white with carpeting—not a vehicle to go hunting in. We tried to explain! Oh well! It was beautiful country, and there was no roadside litter anywhere. Living in Mississippi, we see trash along the highways, and I hate littering, so that was something I noticed quickly. It started snowing as soon as we left the airport. We were truly enjoying the trip as we headed to a little town with one small motel, a general store, a hamburger joint, and a Pizza Hut.

After arriving at the motel, we could tell we were in a target-rich environment (for a game warden). Pulling in, we started to work documenting tag numbers from Louisiana, North Carolina, Pennsylvania, and Texas. We could see guys cleaning ducks near the corner of the motel. Toby and a guide/cameraman greeted us in the parking lot. Toby excitedly said, "The ducks are here, and we been hammering 'em. Y'all brought plenty of shells, didn't ya?" We said, "Yes, and we are ready to start busting caps!" Toby said that we'd leave out about 4:00 a.m. We socialized a bit with the guys cleaning ducks and tried to count what they had, but were unsuccessful. Some were a little cautious with us just pulling up.

After we settled in our room, everyone started gathering in the lobby area, and we soon joined them. As the night progressed and the alcohol started loosening up lips, I could tell that things were going to be overwhelming if half of what they were saying was true. The numbers of ducks and geese they said they had been killing daily was almost hard to believe. After everyone went to their room for the night, Charles and I stayed up for several hours making notes from the conversations we had heard (e.g., names, places, other guys supposedly hunting).

The first morning of our hunt was unbelievable. There were six of us: Charles and me, two hunters from Pennsylvania, Toby, and another guide/cameraman. Toby was having all his hunts videoed to use for advertising, as well as selling the videos. He was planning on having his own television show one day. Charles and I had to keep our hats pulled down as well as try to stay away from the camera. We didn't want to be on video if we could help it.

After the decoys were spread out, we set up in some reeds and cattails. The sky was starting to lighten up in the east, and the ducks began coming in as Toby called. The gunfire started roaring as Toby yelled, "Get 'em!" There was constant gunfire, with consistent splashing as ducks (mallard, gadwall, and other miscellaneous species) hit the water. Charles and I were both shooting, but only occasionally would we actually hit ducks, and we kept up with what we killed.

I had always heard that by the time ducks migrated south, all the dumb ones had been shot! After seeing what took place on our first hunt in North Dakota, I believed it! We could shoot a volley into a flock of ducks and, before they were out of sight, Toby would be calling them back. I had never seen that before. Where I grew up duck hunting in Mississippi, when you shot into a flock of ducks, it was over!

After several hours of constant shooting, we started gathering up ducks and running down wounded ones. We placed the ducks in a pile for several photos with Toby. There were approximately sixty ducks in the pile. Toby told us to each pick out a limit of greenheads, and we would leave the rest in the brush. Exceeding the daily bag limit, as well as want and waste violations, were documented. As we started back to the vehicle, I told the others that I had to use the bathroom and, making it very obvious, grabbed a roll of toilet paper and headed back into the brush. I was able to mark the area on my GPS and also made a big *X* with the toilet paper, as I planned to notify a local game warden, who was aware of our covert investigation, so he could go in after dark and get the ducks that had been discarded.

After making it back to the motel midmorning, some of the hunters from North Carolina were also just arriving. It was obvious from conversations with them that they had had a good hunt as well. Everyone hunting with Toby got in a group, and we took more photos with Charles and I offering to take pictures and, again, always making sure we kept our face down or stood behind another hunter if we happened to be in the photo. Charles and I were able to get some good counts on the North Carolina hunters, as they were breasting ducks at a dumpster behind the building. They definitely had exceeded the limit! From our motel room, we took as many photos of the hunters as we could and made notes of what we were seeing transpire.

After everyone had a little snack, we were headed out again with Toby and the camera guy. Toby said that we would scout out a few more places to hunt over the next several days. As we drove around the farm country, every time we saw a group of ducks close to the road, we would creep and shoot. We did that for several hours, killing another twenty-plus ducks. And the videographer was filming it all! Charles and I were trying to discreetly GPS all the discarded ducks. By the end of the first day, I am sure that our group alone had killed close to a hundred ducks.

By midafternoon, we arrived back at the motel. The other hunters were not present. Undoubtedly, after we left, they, too, had headed back out. Charles and I again went back to our room to get our notes in order and decided that we would make a trip into town to try to reach the local game warden, so we could pass on information to him. The game warden acted as though he didn't believe me when I told him how many ducks were left in the field.

Charles and I decided that the guys from North Carolina were definitely killing over the limit, but we were not able to get an accurate count. It appeared that they were bringing most of their ducks back to the motel and cleaning them; we just hadn't figured out what they were doing with the breasted ducks. They had been hunting for several days when we arrived and only had a few ice chests. That night at the motel, Charles and I starting commenting that, if we kept killing ducks like the first day, we wouldn't be able to store them either, hoping that the North Carolina guys might share where they were keeping theirs; they were a little more talkative but weren't sharing everything.

The following morning, as the sky started getting brighter in the east, found us lying on mats in a cornfield hunting Canada geese. It was a beautiful morning, with snow blowing horizontally across the ground at twenty-five to thirty miles per hour. To say the least, for two southern boys, it was cold! With the constant honking of Canadas, Toby would start calling and small groups would break out of the big flocks, zeroing in on our decoys. As the big Canadas would turn into the wind and cup their wings with their landing gear down, we would all rise up on Toby's command and fire. I was amazed at how far those big birds would get when they straightened up their wings and grabbed the wind. They would be out of range of our 3½" magnums quickly!

It was obvious that Toby was going to get the first shot, and the two guys from Pennsylvania weren't very good shots. Charles and I were taking turns running the camera and shooting. Toby's cameraman had gone with a different group that morning, and Charles and I offered to video. Toby was pleased, as were we; we wanted everything on video. We had both killed our limit within the first couple of volleys, and Toby was killing the majority of the rest, even though he would congratulate the two Pennsylvania guys on their shooting! Charles and I would just shoot up in the air.

We heard several big flocks of sandhill cranes, but never did any come within gun range. They were called "ribeye in the sky," and I did want to taste one. Toby stopped all the shooting when we had a limit (group limit), as I believe he killed all but one of the Canadas that the Pennsylvania guys were claiming, and we had picked off a few mallards that tried to set down among our goose decoys.

That afternoon, we did the same as the day before, driving around creeping up on ducks and even shooting some from the road. Charles or I would try to leave some type of mark where ducks were left to make it easier for the game warden to locate them. The bag limit had been exceeded again on ducks for sure, and we documented everything as best as we could utilizing a GPS.

When we pulled back up to the motel, the North Carolina guys appeared to be packing up. When I asked, they said they would be heading home the following morning. I asked one flat out, expressing a need for Charles and me to store some ducks, "Where y'all been putting all your ducks? We are out of ice chest space." He said, "Paying the fella at the pizza place and putting them in his walk-in cooler." I couldn't believe it; he gave me the fella's name and said, "Tell him I told you, and he will let you leave your ducks there if you pay him." I told Charles that we needed to run into town for some drinks and to make a few phone calls. We asked Toby if they needed anything from the store, as we were going to make a run into town to grab a few things. He said they didn't need anything.

Charles and I located the pizza place and called the US Fish and Wildlife Service agent in North Dakota who was over the investigation. I told him, "The hunters from North Carolina are going to be pulling out in the morning, and they supposedly have ducks stored at the pizza place." The agent said, "You got to be kidding! We'll set up surveillance on the pizza place in the morning. We won't stop them until they cross the state line, assuming they get their ducks." I said, "That sounds good, as they will be far away from us and we have one more day of hunting with Toby and the guys from Pennsylvania." I advised him of all the violations that we had documented. He said that the local game warden had taken his dog to the sites we had told them about and picked up a pile of ducks. I said, "That's great, it's coming together well. I'll call you when we pull out tomorrow and advise you of what we do." After that conversation, Charles and I headed back to the motel, somewhat excited, wondering what would transpire the following day.

Arriving back at the motel, Charles and I tried to watch the North Carolina guys packing and could see they were putting what appeared to be ice chests under all the hunting gear (they were trying to get the ducks they had under all their gear). Toby's camera guy had something come up, and he had to go home. Toby asked if Charles and I would help with the video, due to the cameraman having to leave. Toby had gotten very open to us and was telling everything! We were able to get a lot of his illegal outfitting information from Arkansas, Louisiana, and North Dakota on audiotape during the time we spent at the motel.

The next morning found us on another duck hole, and it was a remake of day one! When the sky started to lighten up, the unmistakable sound of what seemed like hundreds of mallards, along with other miscellaneous species, could be heard, and, as soon as Toby started calling, they were dropping into the decoys. Charles and I were taking turns videoing, which made it easier on us, not being so obvious that we weren't killing ducks. After we got through, we had a brief photo shoot with our pile of ducks. We then sorted out a limit for each, at Toby's direction, and left the rest. I again marked the spot on my GPS, and we headed back to the motel.

Charles and I were packing up to head home when Toby knocked on our door and said someone at the motel had told him that we needed to be careful traveling, because the guys from North Carolina had gotten stopped on the highway, and everything they had was seized (all their hunting gear, guns, and so on, as well as their ducks and vehicle)! Toby was warning Charles and me and laughing about what had taken place, so we knew he didn't suspect anything. We all laughed and said that we weren't taking back any more than was legal. After packing up, saying our goodbyes, and exchanging phone numbers, Charles and I headed out to call and meet with state and federal officers to give them any further information we had.

We found out that the information about the pizza place was true. The officers had watched the North Carolina hunters stop and load numerous cardboard boxes full of cleaned ducks in their vehicle. They tailed them until they crossed the state line, where they had a roadblock set up and pulled them over. According to the state officer, that was the biggest waterfowl case they had ever made. He said, laughing, "We seized everything but their clothes and their dog!"

Charles and I flew home to do reports on all that had transpired during the Arkansas and North Dakota hunts with Toby. The hunters from Pennsylvania and North Carolina, Toby from Louisiana, and the cameraman from Texas were all charged with numerous state and federal waterfowl violations. Toby was also charged with a felony Lacey Act violation due to his operating an illegal guide service in North Dakota and being from another state. The cameraman in Texas had federal search warrants issued on his residence there, where all unedited tapes of the hunts were seized. Neither Charles nor I had to appear in court, as all parties involved were quick to plead guilty after their attorneys were presented with the evidence. Toby's dream of having his own duck-hunting show was short lived, as he was not able to hunt anywhere in the United States for three years as part of his sentencing.

CHAPTER 19

MUDDY CAVIAR

One of the individuals Sammy had introduced to Charles and me was a convicted felon named Ron Whitehead from northern Mississippi. He liked to fish the Coldwater River for paddlefish to obtain eggs, or roe as it is called. In Mississippi, it is illegal to sell paddlefish roe. Charles and I had been trying to get in on the roe market, as there were legal buyers in Arkansas. Sammy had told me that black market roe was going for around $35/pound; the legal price for roe was around $60/pound. One large female paddlefish could easily have five to ten pounds of roe.

Ron was a very quiet person who was hard to get close to, but he had a couple of nephews in their thirties, Buck and Steve, who liked to drink and do drugs. Sammy had mentioned them, saying to stay away from them! He didn't trust them. Both nephews had an Arkansas address, driver's license, and commercial fishing license; they each also had a Mississippi nonresident, commercial fishing license. We felt like they were catching Mississippi paddlefish and taking the roe to Arkansas, where it was legal to sell. Now we just had to prove it.

Normally a drug user (especially of crack cocaine) would generally sell pretty quickly if they were low on funds, so we decided to target Buck and Steve and see if they would lead us to bigger fish! We spent quite a bit of time doing surveillance at some of the boat ramps and located their vehicles. We followed them back to a trailer park near Tunica, Mississippi, and spent several nights watching the trailer park and following them around. Finally, one night they went to one of the casinos on the Mississippi River, which gave us an opportunity to contact them.

Charles and I entered the casino and walked around until we spotted one of them. We played slot machines and kept an eye on Buck, who was not faring well at the blackjack table. When he stepped away from the table, we started talking to him. Charles and I both looked rough and smelled of fish, easy to spot and smell. We asked him if we had seen him at the landing on the Coldwater River when we had been buying some fish, and he perked up. He had been drinking, so that made the conversation easier. Buck said, "Y'all buy fish? What kind?" I said, "Mainly buffalo and catfish this time of year. You been having any luck?" He asked about prices, and we discussed possibly doing some business later, as we exchanged phone numbers.

Charles was playing the slots, acting as though he wasn't paying attention to our conversation. Buck started talking about how he was a good gambler. He told Charles to play a different machine. I pulled a wad of cash from my pocket and handed a $20 bill to Charles. Charles slid the bill into the machine Buck said to play, and after a couple of pulls, Charles hit a payoff of $100.

I told Charles to cash out, but Buck said, "Leave it, you'll hit big!" Charles was looking at me; I said again, "Hit the payout button!" Buck said, "I'm telling you, keep playing, you could win big!" I looked at Buck, then at Charles, and said, "Get the payout! I don't gamble!" Charles cashed out; I handed Buck $20 and put the rest in my pocket. I told Buck that if he needed to move some fish, we would be making a run to Memphis on Friday (it was Wednesday). He said, "I'll holler at you!" Charles and I left the casino.

The following afternoon, we stopped by the landing where Buck and Steve's vehicle was parked with an empty boat trailer. When they came up to the landing, Charles and I acted as though we were about to pull out and then recognized Buck. Charles spoke out the passenger window, "Hey man, y'all had any luck?" He responded, "We got a few." Charles said, "You want to get rid of the catfish? We just need a few to top off a load. Got 100 to 150 pounds?" He said, "Probably." I said, "Let me look at them, don't want them if they been dead long. My buyers won't take 'em."

I dug around in their fish while Charles got out the scales and set them up. After we haggled on the price a bit, we weighed out 138 pounds of fish, and Charles put them in the freezer. When I pulled out that roll of cash, Steve and Buck both seemed to get more social. I said, "Who do I pay?" Buck stepped up and said it didn't matter; they were fishing together. I counted out the amount we agreed on and handed it to Buck, all being recorded with a hidden camera in the taillight.

I could see they had some coolers at the back of the boat and quite a bit of blood, and also some screen wire about a foot square. Paddlefish eggs were pushed through screen to remove the fat, one of several cleaning processes. Fishermen harvesting roe illegally would cut the roe out of the fish as soon as they finished running the net. They would then push the eggs through screen, removing some of the fat, and place the eggs in plastic bags or plastic containers, keeping them cool until they got them home to finish cleaning the eggs and salting them. I asked, "Y'all catching anything other than catfish?" Neither was committal.

I told Charles, we could head on to the Arkabutla Reservoir and pick up roe, and we would then head to Memphis early. I thanked Buck and Steve and said, "Maybe we can do business again next week?" They said, "Just holler when y'all are coming through."

We headed out and hit the highway toward Arkabutla. Once we got on the interstate, we headed to Memphis, where we got a hotel. We started putting together a plan on how we might get those guys to sell roe to us. No doubt they were fishing for roe, and they seemed pretty unconcerned to pull up to a ramp with coolers and a screen visible. Maybe they didn't have any with them at the time. We worked out a plan.

The following Monday, Charles gave Buck a call late at night, hoping he might be under the influence and talk. Charles told him that one of our suppliers had been in an accident and was unable to fish, and did he know anyone we could trust to get us some roe? Buck asked, "How much y'all paying?" Charles asked, "Fresh or salted?" He said, "I would prefer to sell fresh." Charles and Buck discussed price, and they settled with $35 a pound if the product looked good.

Charles asked when they would make another egg run, as we would be making a run through their area on Thursday. He told Buck he would call Wednesday night and let him know an approximate time and where to meet. It looked like our first roe buy from those guys was about to happen.

Everything went well, as Charles contacted Buck. Buck said he would bring what they had to the casino parking lot just after dark and to meet in the parking lot. Only Buck showed that night, and we told him to follow us to the edge of the parking lot. I said, looking at the light poles, "Let's get away from all those cameras, don't need any nosey security guards coming out here."

Buck seemed a bit nervous; he kept looking around as I went through each container, smelling the eggs to make sure they were fresh, and Charles weighed and recorded the weight of each container. Charles said as he calculated, "Thirty-six pounds at $35 a pound is $1,260, even." I stepped over to make sure we were in front of the camera and counted out twelve $100 bills and three $20 bills, counting out loud to make sure it was caught on audiotape in case video didn't get it.

After the purchase, I shook hands with Buck and said, "Hope we can do some more business, tell Steve thanks." As he folded the money and put it in his shirt pocket, he said, "Sounds good, I don't like carrying across the line."

That was good, as it showed that he had been transporting across state lines and knew that it was illegal, so he was clearly predisposed.

Over the next couple of weeks, Charles and I did pretty well with Steve and Buck, making two more good purchases. The last purchase, meeting them at the boat ramp, was kind of funny. We passed Ron as we were turning in to the landing; he was headed out. Charles and I just waved and continued to our meet. After that purchase, Buck asked, "You know Ron?" I said, "Ron who?" He responded, "Ron Whitehead." I said, "Yeah, I've met him before, that looked like him pulling out on the highway." He then said, "Ron told me to invite y'all over to his shop for a little poker game." I said, "We got a delivery to make, might stop on the way back Saturday evening. We'll give you a call." Buck said, "You need to come by, you might be able to do some business with Ron." Steve kind of laughed. I said, "We'll see, we've got to hit the road."

During our trip, I received information from a game warden about some guys fishing for roe a little farther south.

We did our same routine, heading toward the Arkabutla Reservoir, then heading north to Memphis to sell the catfish we had picked up from Sammy and several other commercial fishermen in Mississippi and Arkansas. Charles gave Buck a call on the way back, and we met them at a little fish market near the Tennessee state line (Ron's place). We met, talked a bit, and sat down at the table to play poker.

I told them right off the bat that I wasn't much on gambling, but I would play a hand or two. Charles was a card player and knew the games well, so after I lost about thirty dollars, I told them I was out. Charles continued to play, and I just watched and listened as Ron nonchalantly threw out numerous questions about the roe business. I played him off and could tell that Buck and Steve weren't eager to say much.

Ron was fishing to see if we knew the business, best I could tell. I did my best to act uninterested in him, saying, "We're doing pretty good now. Actually, got some more suppliers south of here, and they can process good. I don't have time to process much, running up and down the road, too time consuming." After about two hours, I told Charles that we needed to hit the road. Ron seemed comfortable with us, and we shook hands and headed out.

Buck called several times the next week, but we put him off, as we were trying to contact the other targets a little farther south on whom we had information. We knew about a couple of bars they frequented and a store where they normally got gas. We tried to focus on those places. It's tough in a rural community going into a bar where everybody knows everybody.

We got a break when one of the targets, Tom Eason, who was in his early twenties, pulled into the gas station with several beavers in the back of his truck.

Charles and I had our trailer with freezers, so I started a conversation about the beavers, to open the door. I told him I could move the beavers: "What are you getting on them?" He responded, "What will you pay?" I said, "Five dollars each whole." He quickly said, "Only if we keep the tails." I said, "That will work. Five dollars for medium and large, three dollars for kits and smalls?" He said, "How many you want? We got eighteen." I was looking in his truck and responded, "Where are the rest?" He said, "They're skinning the others now at the house." I said, "I'll follow you over and see if they want to sell the rest." He said, "Sure, just follow me."

To our surprise, he led us to the other two targets. Turned out they were shooting beavers on the river at night for the bounty. When we pulled up, the group didn't look so happy with their partner, and they definitely didn't know how to skin beaver, as I could see. Tom went over and spoke with an older guy, whom he introduced as Ben, and the other guy, a bit younger, mid-forties, as Jeb, Ben's brother.

After we talked a bit, we settled up, and Charles and I purchased all the beavers. I asked if they minded if we skinned them there and they chunked the carcasses. Tom said, "You going to skin all them beavers now? Sure, I'll haul them off!" When I started skinning the beavers, they watched when I pulled my knives out and went to work. It couldn't have been better when Jeb, laughing, said, "I think he's done that a time or two!"

Charles and I were now their buddies. Even better, Tom started carrying the beaver hides to the freezer for us. We told him to put them in the freezer where we had the paddlefish roe we had just purchased. He knew exactly what all those plastic containers were! We didn't have to mention a thing. By the time we got the last beaver skinned, Tom asked, "Do you buy eggs?" I quickly responded to Charles, acting like I was a little ticked off, "Where has he been putting those hides?"

I changed the subject back to beavers and said, "When y'all going to shoot beavers again? Let me know and I'll stop by if we're in the area." Tom responded, "Just let us know when you're coming through and we'll go the night before." We exchanged numbers and didn't say anything else about the paddlefish roe. I knew it would be better if we took it slow.

The following week, Charles and I were headed out on our route through Mississippi and Arkansas. I gave Tom a call and told him we would be coming through on Wednesday. He said, "Great, we'll try to go Tuesday night! Holler at me Wednesday morning." I said, "I will." The weather turned bad on Tuesday night, so they didn't go, but after calling him Wednesday morning, he asked us to stop by anyway. Charles had had something come up at home, so I went to meet with Tom alone after transporting Charles back to his truck.

I met Tom at a little bar near Batesville, Mississippi. He started introducing me to everyone, like we had been buddies forever. It wasn't long before I realized there was some heavy drug use going on at this little juke joint. By closing time and after many pool games, Tom was wasted. I offered to drive him home, even though I didn't know where that was. He got in my truck and started giving me directions.

We wound up at a house trailer behind a little carwash, near Calhoun. He said, "Let's stop here for a minute, I need to get something." There were several vehicles parked at the trailer, but it didn't appear that any lights were on inside. He said, "Come on in. This is my friend's place, won't take but a minute." The place gave me a bad feeling; I didn't know if I was getting set up or what. I reached under the seat after Tom got out and grabbed my Smith & Wesson .38, dropping it in my coat pocket. I said a quick prayer, asking God to please get me out of this place!

We entered the trailer, and I could make out groups of three or four people huddled up, with the only light source coming from their lighters as they smoked crack. Tom introduced me to the host of this grand abode; it was nasty, no furniture, and we had to step over passed-out individuals to get to his office, one of the bedrooms in the back of the trailer. I didn't quite get his name, due to the loud music playing, when Tom introduced me as his friend. The whole place stank; all I could smell was that dry smell of crack and steel wool burning. How someone could smoke that stuff, I had no idea.

We all squatted on the floor, and the dealer counted out three rocks for Tom. Tom asked if he could borrow some money, as he only had ten dollars. I said, sure, and handed him two twenties. As they were finishing the deal, I said, "I got to go, you going with me?" He quickly responded yes, dropping the three rocks of crack cocaine in the cellophane wrapper of his cigarette pack. We felt our way out of the trailer and back to the truck. I then drove Tom home and helped him to his house. Oh, what a new friend I had made!

Charles didn't return to work for another week, but I was able to go beaver hunting and headlighting deer and rabbits with Tom and a couple of his crack buddies. On one particular night, Tom, one of his upstanding buddies, and I rode around shooting deer and rabbits. The deal was, I got the beavers, deer, racoons, and rabbits, if I bought the crack. According to the law, that was considered a sale via bartering or trade. I purchased $220 worth of crack that night from three different dealers' homes. My Mississippi Bureau of Narcotics friends were going to like this one!

That was one of the longest nights of my career, as it had started raining and we were riding around in my single-cab Ford F-150. The two of them were doing the shooting while steadily smoking crack. They offered, and I told them sternly, "I don't smoke that crap!" I kept an open beer between my legs, and when they would get out to retrieve a downed critter, I would ease it out the window and dump it, continuing to act as though I was drinking. Several hours into the night, the smell from that crack got to me. After they shot a rabbit, I got out of the truck and started throwing my guts up. They just laughed as I told them I had eaten some greasy chicken from one of the local stores.

Tom had been discussing the roe with his cousins and undoubtedly convinced them that I was on the up-and-up. I stayed in the area for the next several days and was able to go with them to run nets on the Mississippi River, making a purchase of about twenty pounds of roe and documenting where they set their nets. I had plenty on them as far as sales go, with narcotics, deer, and rabbits; I also had them for headlighting, setting illegal nets, illegally taking paddlefish, Lacey Act violations, and the sale of a stolen outboard motor. I told the game warden where their nets were, and, a few days later, he and some other officers caught them running the nets and in possession of paddlefish.

Charles returned, and I had the fresh roe from Tom and his cousins; it was time to try to get something on Ron up on the Tennessee line. I had an idea to just stop by and see if he would show us how he processed his eggs, since our last conversation was about processing, and he acted like he did it a little differently. Maybe we would at least get enough evidence for a search warrant; if we could just see paddlefish eggs at his residence, that should be enough.

I gave him a call, and he invited us to stop by; said he was processing some at that time. Great! I was ready to bring this one to a close. Charles and I pulled up at Ron's home, and he greeted us like friends, welcoming us into his house. Walking in, I noticed a gun standing in the corner; it looked like a lever-action rifle. Ron was a convicted felon and was not supposed to be in possession of a gun.

Ron then invited us out behind his shop, where he showed us how he processed his paddlefish eggs. He had numerous eggs in women's panty hose, hanging down about a foot from a tabletop to drain. He went through his curing process in detail, telling how much salt he used, and so on. We were getting it all on audiotape.

We even got a sample of the eggs, as we asked to taste them. Try to keep eggs in your mouth for thirty minutes without them falling to pieces. After we finally got away from Ron and back in the truck, I realized that Charles had tried to do the same thing, as we both were trying to spit eggs into a paper envelope. It wasn't much, but we had enough to get a search warrant!

After leaving Ron's place, I called Special Agent Robert Oliveri of the US Fish and Wildlife Service, telling him what we had and that we needed to get a warrant before he sold his eggs! Agent Oliveri acted on it, and the next

Diving is a common method to illegally harvest mussels. (Photo courtesy of the MDWFP.)

morning, federal agents served a search warrant on Ron's home, shop, and surrounding property. He was taken into custody and charged as a felon in possession of a firearm.

During the next month, Charles, other state and federal agents, and I worked on warrants in Mississippi and Arkansas that would bring Operation Delta and Operation Muddy Caviar to a close. I was ready for a break! Between the two states, we filed more than 150 charges (federal and state, misdemeanors and felonies) and arrested approximately eighty people. Violations included federal felony Lacey Act violations, sale of game and fish, interstate trafficking of illegal game, illegal trafficking in narcotics (sale and distribution), sale of stolen property, headlighting and illegal take (netting paddlefish), and other, minor charges.

Although it took close to six months to close all the cases, we didn't have to go to trial on one single case. All the subjects pleaded guilty to a least some of the charges. I was glad to end that one, as it could have gone on forever. I was ready to cut my hair, shave my beard, and try to stay at home awhile. From the beginning of Operation AST and on to Delta and Muddy Caviar, we had worked almost three years and traveled to nine states: Mississippi, Arkansas, Louisiana, Tennessee, North Dakota, Texas, Pennsylvania, North Carolina, and Kentucky.

CHAPTER 20

HOT AND FULLY AUTOMATIC: OPERATION ROOSTER

While traveling south on Highway 61, I spotted one of those businesses that always interested me. In a small town in the Mississippi Delta, a business that sold guns and hunting supplies was a great place to hang out and listen. This type of business usually drew numerous locals, as well as nonresident hunters visiting the area, to share their hunting tales and drink coffee or beer, depending on the time of day. Those types of places could generate lots of good information and potentially lead to a good case. I had a new covert agent with me and thought that it would be a good place to introduce him to wildlife investigative work.

Greg Johnson had only been with special ops for about three months and had not been able to get anything going. He had transferred from a covert narcotics unit and thought that wildlife investigative work would be a breeze. I told him, after he had made several unsuccessful attempts to purchase wildlife, "Not quite as easy as buying drugs, huh!" He said he couldn't understand; he had people offering to sell him weed, ecstasy, and meth, but when he mentioned a rabbit, deer, or fish, they would clam up! I kind of laughed and asked him, "Would you take a stranger hunting or fishing with you?" He said, "No, and I never thought of it like that, but it makes sense."

We entered the old store; to our left was a wall with nothing but guns, a lot of miscellaneous hunting supplies, and a lot of used junk. Scattered about were a coffeepot, a drink box, and a table with several men laughing and joking. They gave us a good looking-over as I asked about the coffee. Greg went to the gun section and showed an interest in a used deer rifle. As we had discussed before entering, Greg was to do most of the talking, while I listened. As the men's conversation at the table seemed to get back to normal, Greg's interest in the gun had sparked the owner's attention, and he was turning on the charm in hopes of making a sale. Greg had a good knowledge of firearms and was able to carry the conversation well, discussing different calibers, ranges of different firearms, and the like. Greg asked Eddie, the owner, if he could bring a gun by for his gunsmith to work on. Eddie said, "Man yeah, bring it by and let me take a look at it!" Every other sentence, Eddie would reference a rooster; hence, the name of our investigation became Operation Rooster.

Greg shook his hand as we started to leave, but all I did was give the fellow a little nod. Many years of law enforcement experience told me that something was up at that place. As Greg and I discussed the number of used guns for sale, we agreed something wasn't right. In a rural area like that, you wouldn't think they would have so many used guns, so much equipment.

I told Greg that we would take it slow and spend a little time hanging out there to try to become one of the guys. He agreed, with a bit of excitement in his voice. Most of the time, you could find out a lot more if you played dumb and let the target show off with his knowledge. We planned that I would not go back in, since Greg and Eddie had hit it off so well. Over the next several months, Greg stopped by at least once a week, letting Eddie work on a gun and making some small purchases. Greg had thrown out the subject of automatic weapons in conversation, and Eddie grinned and laughed, saying, "I can convert if you ever need it." Greg did well and didn't jump on it, just letting the conversation flow on, recording everything.

We decided that I would pose as a fish buyer friend of Greg's who was a little on the shady side, transporting goods to Memphis weekly. Greg was to be the one who ran his mouth too much, hoping to impress Eddie by telling him about all the illegal contraband I carried while transporting fish. On the next contact with Eddie, I was pulling a large, enclosed trailer, and Greg was riding with me. We stopped at Eddie's business, and it was evident that he wanted to know what I had in the trailer, as he continued to ask about it, and where we were going. I would just change the subject, hoping to tweak his curiosity even more.

Greg and I set up a staged transfer of goods at Eddie's business, planning an opportunity for him to see in the trailer. Greg had been at Eddie's business for a bit when I called his cell phone, letting him know I was getting close and that our meeting was set. Eddie was listening to Greg's end of the conversation. Greg said that he had picked up the stuff for me and told me to just stop at Eddie's place, and he would give it to me. As Greg closed his cell phone, Eddie asked, "That your buddy?" Greg responded, "Yeah, he's making a run to Memphis, and I picked up something for him." Eddie was very inquisitive, but Greg said just enough to make him even more eager to know what was going on.

I pulled the enclosed trailer into the large gravel parking lot at Eddie's business, stopping over to one corner, visible but not where anyone pulling in could see in the trailer if I opened it. At the office that morning while prepping, Greg and I had loaded several long, wooden boxes used for transporting guns, and some smaller boxes, all locked. We also placed numerous ice chests full of only ice, duct taped so they couldn't be opened, so as to appear that we were hauling fish. Only one of the boxes actually had guns, an assortment of hunting rifles and several military-style firearms, ARs, and the like.

I exited the vehicle, looking around a moment, then went and unlocked the trailer. I entered the trailer and was moving things around, just making noise. I could hear gravel crunching, so I peeked out of the trailer to see Greg going to his truck. I watched as he removed two guns and started my way. Eddie was watching from the front window of the store. Greg and I shook hands, and we both entered the trailer. Greg whispered, with a little laugh, "He's anxious." We started talking louder; I heard gravel crunching as someone approached.

Loudly enough to be overheard, I told Greg, "We need to hit the road if we're going to make it to Memphis before dark." Greg exited the trailer as Eddie was almost to the corner. He and Greg both stepped around the corner of the trailer as I was putting the last gun in the box. As I turned and saw them, I quickly shut the box, purposely allowing Eddie to see the firearms, and then closed it, also placing a lock on the box.

As I almost had to push him back to close the door on the trailer, Eddie started asking questions. He asked, "Do you buy guns?" I said, "No, I just haul them for a guy, I just buy fish." Eddie quickly responded, "Tell him I got plenty of guns if he wants some more business." I told him I would let him know. I said, "He just pays me to pick up and haul, and I don't ask any questions." Eddie then launched into a long story about how a state police officer in Louisiana had stopped him for speeding while he had a trunkful of guns. He said with a laugh, "I would still be in jail if he had looked in that trunk. You tell your friend I know the business and can move some weapons!" I responded, "I'll tell him, but he's careful."

Greg asked if he could leave his truck in the parking lot until we came back through that night. Eddie responded, "Sure." I told Greg, "I got to go, got another stop to make." We shook Eddie's hand, climbed into the truck, and pulled out, headed north up the highway. After traveling several miles, we pulled over and quickly shut down the video recorder in the trailer, making a few notes on audiotape before turning the recorder off.

Greg and I then headed to the interstate and continued north to Grenada, making sure we were not followed. Greg said, "He's wantin' in bad!" We both laughed about how Eddie seemed to be the boss around those parts. He was very boastful about how he wasn't concerned with the law. Greg said that Eddie's brother and another guy seemed to be talking drugs, as he heard them mention smoking crack and doing other drugs while in Eddie's store. He overheard them say that they would sure be glad when deer season was over, and all the hunters went home.

We decided to throw out something about automatic weapons at Eddie the next time Greg went through, to see what he would say. Greg and I waited until about 10:00 p.m. to head back to get his truck, and we pulled into Eddie's parking lot around midnight. Greg and I then parted ways. I spent the next several days doing reports, running tags, and getting driver's license photos and other information from all the intelligence Greg had been gathering at Eddie's business.

After a week had gone by, Greg stopped by Eddie's shop to chat. Right off the bat, Eddie started asking questions about my business. Greg told him that I said my guy was interested in some fully automatic guns, but he would not deal with Eddie since he did not know him. Eddie said he understood. Greg told Eddie that if he had any, he wanted to move and to let him know, and he would pass that on to me.

Eddie responded, "What does he want, I got a bunch!" Greg said, "AKs, M16s." Eddie said, "I got 'em all!" Greg responded, "Fully auto?" Eddie nodded yes. Greg said, "I'll tell him and holler back at you." Eddie came back, "I got all kinds of stuff to move, if you know what I mean." Eddie then took Greg to the back of the building and opened a door to another large room. Greg said, "My gosh!" as he looked at all the hunting and other gear. There were boots, clothes, boxes of all kinds of ammo, duck decoys, boat winches, radios, televisions, and fishing gear, all in piles. Eddie just laughed: "Like I said, I got plenty to move."

After Greg told me what he'd seen, we met with the assistant US attorney, John Dowdy, and decided that we would set up a surveillance team on the property as well as continuing with covert contact. We also decided that we would try to purchase a fully automatic weapon and see how it went. Greg called Eddie, telling him that my guy wouldn't purchase from him, but if I trusted Eddie, he would just reimburse me. Eddie said he was good with that as long as he got his money. Greg told him we would purchase a fully auto AK-47, and that we would have to test-fire it before I would buy. We set the deal for the following Friday evening.

We did the surveillance from a camper that we placed in a small trailer park near the business. My guys had a boat, and we would swap out every other day. One agent would stay in the trailer, unable to leave for up to forty-eight hours, and he would not be able to make much noise, as there were others in the area and everybody knew each other. It was a long two days! We had a camera with a telephoto lens and a spotting scope to record tag numbers and get descriptions of individuals coming and going from Eddie's business. We tried to make it appear as if no one was at the trailer except when the boat was there. The agent in the trailer could also document Greg and I as we came and went.

Greg called Eddie on Friday morning and asked if he was still good on the AK. Eddie said, "Come on and we'll go shoot!" Greg said we would be there around 1:00 p.m. We photographed the money that would be used in the purchase (four $100 bills and five $20 bills) for evidence. Eddie had told Greg that he would sell the fully automatic AK for $450. We double-checked all audio and video equipment to make sure it was working and hit the road.

About five miles down the road from Eddie's business, we pulled over, turned on all recorders, and stated our names along with the date and time, then continued on to Eddie's store. Neither Greg nor I said anything else until we pulled into Eddie's shop. I asked Greg what time it was, to get an audible recording of our time exiting the vehicle.

As we entered Eddie's business, he seemed a little nervous and was carrying on about a 7 mm magnum he'd been doing some trigger work on. He brought the 7 mm from behind the counter and showed it to me. He pulled the bolt back, dumped four rounds from the gun, then handed it to me, saying, "Pull that trigger and see how smooth it is!" My instinct was to open the bolt and check to see if it was empty, but I'd just watched him empty it, and the whole time he was saying, "Squeeze the m#@#$# f**)&##!"

Greg was to my right and behind me with no one else in the store. I raised the 7 mm mag to my shoulder, pointing at the glass door at the front of his store, and I could see the grocery store across the street. I looked through the scope, raising the gun high until I could see nothing but blue sky and a couple of power lines. The whole time, Eddie was saying, "Pull it!"

I squeezed the trigger. With a *kaboom!!!!!!*, the front door glass shattered and Eddie said incredulously, "I unloaded the m#@#$# f**)&##!" I handed Greg the gun and grabbed Eddie by the shirt, wanting to beat his face in and thinking the law would be rolling up any minute! I said, "Undoubtedly it wasn't unloaded, you fool!" He started laughing and said, "Let's go, the AK's in my truck."

Eddie quickly placed duct tape on the glass to hold what was still there. He was laughing and said, "That's not the first time!" A young man who had been hanging around the store walked up to the door where I was standing and said, "What happened?" I said, "It was a big red wasp, but I got him!" Eddie, laughing, stepped out of the store and headed to his truck, saying, "Y'all follow me, come on!"

Greg and I got into our truck and pulled out, following Eddie. Greg was about to bust laughing, and I was mad as a hornet, pointing to my recorder. We didn't need to talk, as we were still recording. We followed Eddie just out of town to a bridge over a small ditch, where he pulled over and exited his vehicle. He had a Chinese-made AK-47 with a banana clip. I asked if it was fully auto. He handed the gun to me and said, "Let her rip, and it's loaded, ha!"

I stepped into the back of my truck, as there was a video camera in the toolbox that would get everything on video. I aimed the AK into the ditch and squeezed the trigger. The fully auto's *dat, dat, dat, dat, dat* echoed up the ditch, as I sprayed several bursts into the water. I handed it to Greg and said, "You try it." He did the same until he emptied the magazine.

Eddie excitedly said, "what do you think about that m#@#$# f**)&##?" I responded, "I like it, but it's not for me. Are we good on a price?" Eddie said, "Four hundred fifty dollars, nothing less, and that's cheap!" I responded, "Like I said, it's not for me, but if he likes it, I'm sure he will want to do more business with you. I don't need any trouble!" Eddie said, "You don't have to worry about anything around here!"

I pulled my wallet out, handed Eddie $450, and told him to count it. He behaved perfectly and counted it out loud, then folded the money and placed it in his shirt pocket. We shook hands while Greg was placing the gun in our truck, then he and Greg shook hands. Eddie said, laughing, as he got into his truck, "I guess I better go fix my door."

Greg and I stated the time and cut our recorders off. Then, as we drove up the highway, we discussed what had transpired. I was concerned about the accidental discharge of the 7 mm mag at the store. I had never had an unloaded gun fire! I contacted the assistant US attorney who was over the case and told him what had happened. He laughed and said, "Put it all in the report." Our first illegal fully auto purchase, and the front door of the store was shot out! I guess it went well, but I was still worried about that bullet. In fact, couldn't sleep that night for thinking about it.

The following morning, I gave Eddie a call just to make sure everything was good. When Eddie answered the phone, he seemed very nervous and said, "It's bad, I can't talk now, I'll call you back!" He then hung up. That didn't help me any. I gave him an hour; when he didn't call back, I called him. He answered and said, laughing, "You ain't gonna believe what you f*&^&*# did!"

The laugh helped me, but I said, "What's going on?" He said, "When you fired that f*&^&*# 7 mag, you hit that big fiber optic line on the power pole, and they've been in here asking me questions about the hole in my front door!" I laughed, silently thanking God, because I then knew what happened to the bullet. He said he told them that he didn't know anything about the line, also stating, "They said it knocked out eight hundred homes from phone and internet service!" Laughing, he said, "They know the bullet came from here, but I know them fellas, they don't care. Your man like that AK?" I answered, "Yeah, but he isn't wanting to do business directly. If you have any more, he can move them."

Eddie said, "Great, I got quite a few and will be getting more." I told him that Greg and I would be driving through the following week, and we could talk then.

The surveillance guys had been getting a lot of movement in and out of the store, but due to the vehicles driving around back, they could not identify what was being moved. No doubt they were up to a lot more than drinking coffee and working on guns for local hunters. We felt that Eddie's brother and the guy who hung out with him were probably stealing stuff and that Eddie was moving it through his store. It was evident from what Greg had learned while hanging out at Eddie's place that they were also moving drugs. We just couldn't prove it. It was time for Greg and I to bump things up a bit!

We decided to go to Eddie's place and start talking a little more, since we had one buy under our belt and nothing had happened. Greg and I visited Eddie and set up to purchase a fully auto .30 caliber carbine rifle. Eddie showed it to us, and I told him to just hold onto it until I made the next run. I explained that I did not want to tie my money up too much, as I just got paid so much to deliver. He said, "I got a fully auto M16 if he wants it, and plenty of other guns that I'll make him a deal on if he can move them." I asked what kind, and he said, "Hunting rifles and shotguns." I said, "I'll let him know." Eddie's brother and his running buddy had entered the store while Eddie and I were talking. Eddie never shut up, so I didn't either; they could easily hear what we were saying.

Greg grabbed a drink and started talking to Bobby, Eddie's brother. Bobby had normally been kind of quiet but appeared to be under the influence then, either stoned or somewhat intoxicated. He started telling Eddie that they were going to have to move everything he had at his trailer, because he had been told that "they" (meaning law enforcement) were going to do a search warrant in the next couple of days. That was good to know, as we already knew they had contacts with some of the local law enforcement and Eddie at one time had been a local justice of the peace (i.e., a county judge). No one except the feds knew that Greg and I were working covertly in the area.

Bobby laughed as he talked about all the guns he and his buddy had been stealing from deer camps up and down the Mississippi River. We were able to get it all on tape as they laughed about how a game warden had gotten after them one night and they had escaped in a four-wheeler they had stolen from one of the hunting camps. They bragged of how and where they were hiding stolen property, from guns to vehicles. They also elaborated about how a particular mechanic was helping them by stripping vehicles and rolling back odometers. After that afternoon, we knew we had enough information through surveillance and covert contacts to secure arrests as well as obtain search warrants for the business and at least two other properties. We wanted to make one more illegal purchase before bringing it to a close.

The following week, Greg and I purchased the fully auto .30 caliber carbine and also obtained some information from the young man who worked in the building next to Eddie's place. The young fellow was apparently addicted to crack cocaine, as the few times we had been near him we could always smell it. On that particular day, as Greg and I were waiting for Eddie to come open up the shop, the guy started telling us how he had watched Bobby and Hub, Bobby's partner, cut a man up and put him in bags. He was evidently scared. I acted as though I didn't really believe his story, and he said, "No, I watched them and then they loaded the bags into the truck. They made me go with them and told me that's what happens to folks that cross them. While driving through the hills in Yazoo County, they threw bags out into the deep gullies along the road." He said they did it in the kitchen at Hub's place and that blood was everywhere: "They just chopped him up!"

As Eddie pulled up, the guy quit talking and walked back to the other building. After paying Eddie for the carbine, Greg and I hung out at Eddie's place talking about making future purchases with a little bigger volume. Bobby and Hub came in laughing and joking about how the Mississippi Bureau of Narcotics had searched Bobby's place and found nothing. He told Eddie, "They walked all over the stuff and didn't get a thing. I bet they don't have a rat anymore, either!"

I didn't trust Bobby too much, as he looked crazy. Greg and I both felt it was getting time to bring the covert portion of Operation Rooster to a close. We got with the assistant US attorney and worked out the affidavits for arrest and the search warrants. The plan was to set up another purchase from Eddie and do a buy-bust, where Greg and I would get arrested as well, to try to protect our cover until court. As soon as the bust went down, the ATF agents and state game wardens would execute search warrants at three addresses simultaneously.

Over the next week, we had a lot to do, including several meetings to brief state and federal law enforcement supervisors and decide how to handle the information received about the alleged John Doe who had been dismembered and disposed of somewhere in Yazoo County. We picked teams to do search warrants and the buy-bust takedown. The teams would be notified of the meeting place only on the night prior to the buy-bust. We had a group of trusted officers, handpicked over the years, who executed all our search warrants. These state game wardens were the best I knew of any law enforcement group, state or federal, in search warrant execution.

We decided that we would arrest only Eddie first, and possibly Bobby, depending on what was found at Bobby's residence during the search. We didn't have enough to get an arrest warrant immediately. He'd brought the carbine into the shop the day we purchased it from Eddie, but the surveillance guys only saw him carry "what appeared to be the carbine" into the store just before we arrived and could not positively say that it was the gun we purchased.

On the morning of the takedown, the teams met at 4:00 a.m. to get their final briefing and set up locations to sit and wait for the signal to execute. Greg and I contacted Eddie by phone at 7:00 a.m. to let him know we would be there at 7:30. Greg called him the night before to let him know we were coming through early because we had some other pickups. We wanted as few people there as possible. Greg and I were in my truck pulling the same trailer we had been using, with two federal agents inside.

Greg and I pulled into the parking lot on time, and Eddie was waiting. After a little talking, he led us to the back room of the store to show us the M16. Greg and I each looked at the gun; Greg removed the magazine and checked to make sure it was unloaded while I was counting out $600. We were both wearing wires, so the takedown team, as well as the agents in the trailer, knew everything that was happening.

After paying Eddie, Greg took the gun and we made our way to the front of the store. I asked Eddie if he would help us load some stuff into the trailer from the truck. He said, "Sure," as he put the money into his pocket. We wanted him away from any firearms when he was arrested. I had an ice chest full of ice that was taped shut, and I asked him to help me put in the trailer. Eddie grabbed one end of the heavy ice chest, I the other, and we made our way to the back of the trailer. Time always seemed to slow down at this point in an operation!

As I opened the door of the trailer and stepped away from the opening, all I could hear was, "Federal agents, on the ground! On the ground!" Eddie's eyes were like pie plates, and he went to the ground, but wouldn't let go of the ice chest! One of the agents handcuffed Eddie and the other took off after a young man who had come from the other building as we were walking toward the truck. Greg and I both eased around behind the trailer as vehicles full of state and federal officers covered the place to secure the store.

They took photos of the M16 after it was tagged, along with the money that had been paid for the gun, which they had removed from Eddie's pocket. He was read his Miranda rights and escorted back into the store. I heard on an officer's radio, "We got the main target, execute warrants." The rush of activity was slowing when one of the agents came up to Greg and I and said, "Good one, there's a pile of stuff in that place!"

Eddie's arrogance was all he had left, but even his bold character shriveled as he watched gun after each gun being removed from behind the counter and inventoried by its serial number. Greg and I showed them the back room and around the back of the building, where there were vehicles, ATVs, all sorts of hunting gear, and ammo that had been stolen from numerous hunting camps.

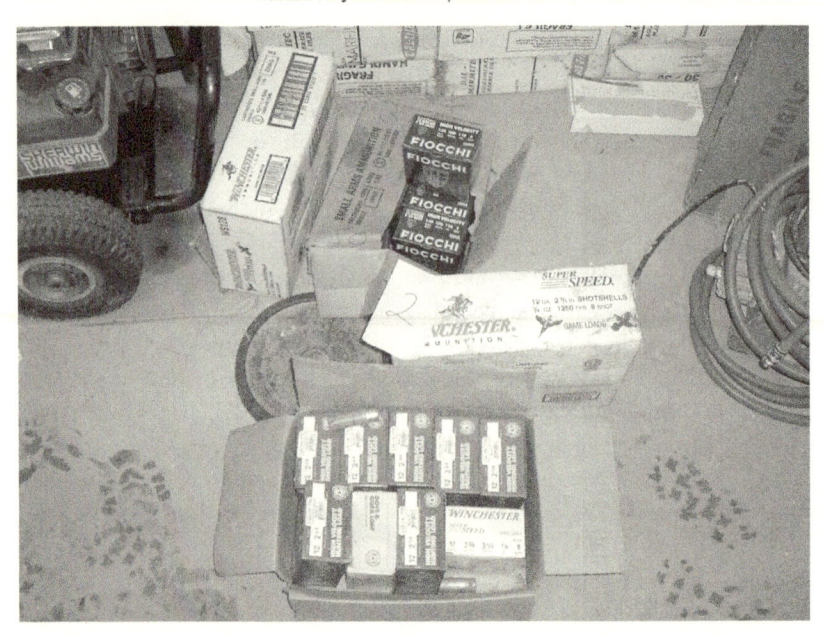

Stealing hunting equipment and ammunition from hunting camps was common. (Photo courtesy of the MDWFP.)

A stolen vehicle is being dismantled. (Photo courtesy of the MDWFP.)

The team that went to Bobby's place seized numerous firearms and narcotics as well as other items to be checked later. We only made two arrests that day. With more than one hundred guns seized, we had to call wreckers to haul off the vehicles and ATVs.

Eighteen months of hard work had paid off in the apprehension of some guys who thought they could beat the system. A lot of interviews followed, with Eddie pleading guilty to illegal firearms charges and going to federal prison for four years. Before Bobby ever went to court, he killed his wife, who had left him, and then took his own life. We were never able to locate any remains of the John Doe who had supposedly been killed and dismembered. It took several months to get the guns we had retrieved back to their rightful owners; many were kept by the state because no one had ever reported them as stolen.

The best outcome from the case took place after Eddie got out of prison; I was told that he went to a local church and related the story of what he had done, asking for forgiveness. God is good!

CHAPTER 21

BLACK MARKET BUCKS

After receiving an anonymous tip that an individual who had a permitted high-fence enclosure was importing deer from out of state, I discussed the matter with US Fish and Wildlife Service Special Agent Robert Oliveri. We then consulted with the US attorney's office and decided to investigate it further. Agent Oliveri and I drove up to the high-fence enclosure, near Itta Bena, Mississippi, to do some surveillance. We followed the gravel county road that ran along the fence and noticed one large buck with what appeared to be a tag in his ear. Due to the distance, we weren't 100 percent sure.

As we were driving by, several other vehicles slowed to look at and photograph the deer inside the fence. The deer we were looking at did not seem wild. Agent Oliveri dropped me off and I watched the gate for several hours, getting a few pictures of some vehicles entering the fenced-in area and checking feeders. I did see a man who fit the driver's license photograph of Richard Johnston, the owner of the property and permit holder with the Mississippi Department of Wildlife, Fisheries, and Parks.

The following week when Agent Oliveri and I conducted another drive-by, the entire fence along the county road had black visqueen from top to bottom. I guess he got tired of all the people looking at his large deer! I imagine the tip came from some of those onlookers, as they mentioned tags in several deer, although we never could confirm it. We did notice a sign about guided waterfowl hunts—"Johnston's Guided Duck Hunts"—in front of a nice lodge on the side of the highway not far from the high fence. We decided that I would contact him covertly and set up a duck hunt, to see if we could possibly find out more about his deer operation.

I called the number on the sign, and Richard Johnston answered the phone. I inquired about a duck hunt and prices. After a little discussion, I booked a duck hunt. The hunt was for pen-raised mallards. The following month found me sitting in a blind with a guide and another hunter named Dr. Sithe, who was from Georgia. I have been on a lot of undercover hunts before, but this was the first one with pen-raised ducks. They had an old oxbow lake where they had released hundreds of mallards. As it got daylight, I could hear a boat at each end of the lake that sounded like they were running in circles. The boat drivers were trying to flush the ducks toward us. We were at the middle of the lake in an open area, with our guide calling away. It wasn't but a few minutes later and we had mallards flying in from both directions just above the water. It only took a few minutes, and I had my four ducks. The guide told me to shoot all I wanted for $15 a duck. I told him, "Four is enough for me. I'll just watch Dr. Sithe! I'm enjoying this." I started talking about big deer, and he said, "If you're interested in killing a big deer, you need to talk to Mr. Johnston."

After our hunt, while the guide was cleaning our ducks, Mr. Johnston stopped by to see how our hunt went. The doctor and I both acted as though we had enjoyed it. I told him that I was interested in killing a 180+ Boone and Crockett buck and that the guide said he might be able to help me. He said, "I might. Got some pretty nice bucks on my place." I asked if he had any photographs. He kind of laughed and said, "I do at my office. Stop by when you head out," and he gave me directions on how to get there.

After lunch, I stopped by Johnston's office to view some photos of deer on his place. I had my recorder going. He was very boastful about some of his bucks. The photos he showed me had names on the back. I picked out a large ten-point and asked, "Do you think I might be able to get a shot at that one?" He said, "If you're in the right stand you should be able to." I then stated, "I don't really have long to hunt. You think we could make it happen? How much?" I was still looking at the photo. He said, "For $10,000, I bet you'll get a shot." I said, "I would love to have him in my office!" He said, "I bet he would look nice there!" I asked, "How long do I have, before I let you know?" He said, "First come, first served. Deer season will be open in another month." I said, "I'll let you know something in a few days." He said, "Look forward to seeing you again."

I left his office and quickly pulled over down the road and wrote down the names of the deer. I did notice tags in a couple of the photos. I remembered something about a guy looking for live deer for sale during Operation Cold Storage; I needed to look back through my files. I checked with a wildlife biologist concerning tagged deer in high-fence areas. He said that the only places that should have tagged deer would be several high-fence operations where

Mississippi wildlife biologists were conducting studies. I passed that information on to Agent Oliveri and put together a report on what I had learned during the duck hunt.

We carried our information to the US attorney's office and applied for a search warrant of Johnston's home, office, duck camp, outbuildings, vehicles, computers, and high-fence area. The judge signed it, so Agent Oliveri and I put together three teams to execute the warrants and interview anyone contacted while serving the warrants, including guides. The teams were made up of both state and federal agents.

During the execution of the search warrants, Agent Oliveri interviewed Richard Johnston; Johnston was very arrogant and denied bringing deer into Mississippi. We also interviewed a man John who worked for Mr. Johnston. He wouldn't admit to seeing any deer but did say that he had seen a white F-150 pickup from Louisiana with a livestock trailer pull into the high-fence area after dark a few times. He lived on the county road that went along the high fence. When asked about deer with tags in their ears, he said, "I've seen some, but I didn't ask any questions."

After getting everything loaded up three hours later, we headed back to the office and spent the next month going through documents and interviewing other individuals. We did find a handwritten list of names with dollar amounts next to them. Two of the names listed were on the back of the photographed deer Johnston had shown me! There were also several names with Louisiana phone numbers.

After contacting the individuals in Louisiana, we decided we needed a formal interview with several of them. We contacted the Louisiana Department of Wildlife and Fisheries and several federal agents to help us. After running down all the names we had, we made a hit when we pulled up at one house that had a white F-150 pickup with a gooseneck cattle trailer attached. The slots on the trailer were boarded up. We met with a Jonas Batholem, who raised captive deer, which was legal to do in Louisiana. After a little time with him, he admitted to transporting numerous deer to Johnston's place in Mississippi.

We continued the investigation in Mississippi. I contacted one of the leading professors on white-tailed deer at that time at one of the colleges. I told him what I was looking into and asked him if anyone by the name of Johnston had called about deer. He acted kind of funny and said that something had just come up, and that he would call me back. I said, "Just call when you have a minute." I wasn't asking any questions that I thought would implicate him. I continued calling people, following up on leads that we had uncovered. One individual who owned a high fence told me really quickly, "If you didn't know that guy that does all the research at the college, you can't get any help."

I was baffled at first, so I called Agent Oliveri and said that we might need to go talk to that deer professor at the college. He said, "Let's go see what he's got to say." Several days later, we drove to the college but could not find the professor. We went up the ladder a bit and spoke with the administrator of the college. He said that the professor had turned in his resignation the day prior, saying that it was a family emergency, and left. That threw us a curve.

Oh well, we had a good felony Lacey Act case against Johnston and Batholem in Louisiana. Batholem pleaded guilty in Louisiana to a misdemeanor Lacey Act violation due to his cooperation. Johnston got a lawyer and dragged things out for several more months, but finally pleaded guilty to one felony count of violating the Lacey Act. He lost his high-fence permit, and all the tagged deer were removed later by wildlife biologists of the MDWFP. He paid a hefty fine of $10,000, along with losing his hunting privileges for three years. Because of the felony conviction, he could not possess a firearm for the rest of his life. If he was caught in possession of a firearm, he would be looking at a minimum of five years in a federal penitentiary.

CHAPTER 22

WILD TURKEYS FOR SALE

One unique investigation started when a game warden called me and asked if one could tell the difference between a domestic turkey and a wild one. At first, I said, "Sure!" Then I said, "Let me double-check on that and I'll call you back." After doing a little research, I found out there was no test that would positively identify a wild turkey from a domestic turkey—that is, a domestic turkey that looks like a wild turkey, not a white one. I called the warden back and told him what I had found. He didn't say anything else about it.

I received another call from someone saying they had seen an advertisement for wild turkeys for sale in the *Market Bulletin*, a paper published by the Mississippi Department of Agriculture and Commerce where you could advertise the selling of anything from land to livestock to farm equipment and more. To follow up, I purchased a *Market Bulletin*. Sure enough, there it was in the poultry section, "Wild Turkeys for Sale" and a phone number.

Over the years, I have had people tell me that one should be able to incubate turkey eggs and put the young birds back into the wild once they have hatched, but not sell them for personal profit. Wildlife biologists state that one can't raise turkeys in a pen and then release them due to a variety of diseases that wild turkeys can catch when they are so close together. These diseases could spread to a larger number of birds.

I got my recorder and called the number. A Mr. Duncan answered the phone. I told him I wanted to get some turkeys to restock our hunting club. I asked, "Are they wild or domestic? Can they fly?" He came back, "They are wild and can fly." We discussed prices, and I said, "Let me talk with the hunting club and I'll call you back." After getting off the phone, I contacted my supervisor, Don

Brazil, and told him the situation. We decided that we would set up a buy and see what happened.

I called Mr. Duncan back and asked when a good time would be to come purchase some turkeys. I told him I wanted a few gobblers and six hens. He said, "No problem, but you'll have to come after 5:00 p.m. or on Saturday." We set up a meeting for Saturday.

My partner, Greg Johnson, went with me, and we made the purchase. Mr. Duncan greeted us wearing a US Forest Service uniform shirt. We were able to get good video and audio footage of the purchase and noticed that he had quite an operation. After we made the purchase, I asked, "How do you get these turkeys?" He said, "I work for the Forest Service, and when we work fires in the spring, I go back and try to find the eggs and incubate them." I asked, "We won't get in trouble for this, will we?" He laughed and said, "Far as I'm concerned, they are domestic turkeys now." He said, "Just be careful who you talk to, but I've been doing it for years."

Well, we knew what was going on, and undoubtedly a lot of other folks did, too! I went back to the office and told Don about the situation, asking what he wanted to do. He said, "If he is collecting wild eggs, that's a violation of the law, and if he's selling them, that's a violation, too. He needs to be stopped." I mentioned the fact that he worked for the Forest Service and that it might get uncomfortable. We decided that we would get a group of officers and biologists to visit Mr. Duncan, make a buy-bust, and seize all the turkeys. We would take the turkeys to Mississippi State University for care until any court decision.

We set up the buy-bust the following week, and everything went smoothly. Mr. Duncan was arrested and charged with the sale of game animals. We contacted the US Forest Service, and they got involved as well. We did take a little heat from some of the locals, who stood behind Mr. Duncan, saying he was saving turkeys that would have just died. After the Forest Service investigators got through with their side of the investigation, they allowed Mr. Duncan to retire and keep his retirement benefits if he pleaded guilty to the charge of illegal sale of wildlife. There were a lot of people who wanted to testify on his behalf if he went to trial. I guess retirement was preferable to feeding his pride.

CHAPTER 23

DUCK HUNT WITH MY DENTIST

US Fish and Wildlife Service Special Agent Robert Oliveri (Bob) and I had planned a covert teal hunt with a guide in Issaquena County, Mississippi. Bob had received information that the outfitter was allowing hunters to kill more than their legal limits. He had set up the hunt, and I was going to help document it.

We met not far from the outfitter's headquarters on the highway. I followed Bob to the camp. We arrived at approximately 5:00 a.m.; Bob was still doing something at his truck when I entered the camp and introduced myself to the outfitter. I saw six hunters and immediately overheard one of them talking about Bob and a run-in he'd had with him the previous hunting season. I was talking with the guide, watching for Bob to come through the door any second! I told the guide that I had left my wallet in the truck and eased back out the door, hoping to catch Bob before he entered and our cover was blown.

Bob was still at the truck, thankfully! I told him the situation, and we decided it would be best if he "had an emergency and had to leave." Bob got in his truck and left. I went back in the camp and told the guide that Bob had an emergency at home and had to leave, something about one of his kids. The guide appeared sympathetic and said to tell him to call and reschedule a hunt. I said, "I will." Wow, that was close!

I heard a voice in the corner of the camp that sounded very familiar. I peeked past the fella I was talking to, and it was my dentist! I hadn't seen him in several years, so hopefully he wouldn't recognize me. My appearance had changed quite a bit, as I now had long hair and a beard. I dodged him as long as I could at the camp, while everyone was getting ready to hunt.

We left the camp shortly after I arrived. I was riding with one of the guides and two other hunters. After we pulled up to the abandoned catfish pond where we were going to hunt, the other guide pulled up and dropped off a hunter to go with us, my dentist! It was still dark, and we all started sloshing through the knee-deep water to the blind.

I did everything I could to keep from getting too close to the dentist. We got in the blind, and fortunately there was a hunter between us. Then that hunter had to go hit the bushes to take care of a bodily urge, and when he returned, the dentist slid over right beside me. Thankfully he was fired up about the hunt and was staring into the horizon looking for ducks. I could remember when I used to go to him, while I was a game warden, that he was always talking about hunting and asking me questions while he had dental instruments in my mouth.

As the colors of the morning sky started to brighten, you could hear the whistling of teal zipping by, and, oh, he was excited. The guide was calling, and upon his command we all started firing. I was just shooting in the direction of the ducks, not wanting to kill any teal. It was pretty fast shooting for about forty-five minutes. When things started slowing down, my dentist tried to talk, and I pretended that I didn't hear him. I finally had to talk a little to keep from appearing rude. After a few minutes of talking, he said, "Have we met before? You seem familiar." I said, introducing myself, "I don't believe so."

It appeared that he may have shot over the limit of teal, but due to the other hunters, I couldn't be sure. I did see him knock down a couple of shovelers that were not retrieved. I was sure the guide had killed over the limit, but due to the other two hunters sitting between us, I would have had a hard time with that case. It was actually very humorous. I hope that my dentist reads this one day!

CHAPTER 24

CHAMPION TRAP SHOOTER!

It was late August and getting close to dove season when I received a call from US Fish and Wildlife Service Special Agent Robert Oliveri (Bob). He wanted me to covertly contact two people—Mike and John Steverson—whom we had been getting information on concerning waterfowl violations. They were supposedly guiding duck hunts west of Greenwood, Mississippi. Bob had received a tip that the Steverson brothers had a well-known champion trap shooter, Bart Sikes, coming down from Iowa to dove hunt with them. Trap shooting is a type of competitive shooting of shotguns at clay targets launched from a throwing device. It is a lot of fun.

Talk about taking a shot in the dark! I was not too interested, as it just didn't seem like much to go on, but I knew that Bob had good sources and I trusted his judgment. I told him I would try. Bob gave me a phone number for Mike Steverson. After getting my story straight in my head, I gave Mike a call.

Mike answered the phone, and I told him that a friend at a recent wildlife extravaganza in Jackson had told me that he guided duck hunts. He immediately went into sales mode. I asked, "Do y'all have teal hunts?" He responded, "We hadn't planned on any, but we might." He told me about the type of duck hunts they normally had and described their camp, the lodging, and the food they served. I told him I hadn't duck hunted in several years and was just wanting to get some information from a couple of different guides before I booked a hunt. He continued to try to sell me on their operation and the numbers of ducks they normally killed.

Toward the end of our conversation, I said, "Do y'all have any or do you know of any good dove hunts?" He responded, "We'll go somewhere, but we don't really have anything planned. Come go with us, we'll find some birds. No charge! We can discuss a possible duck hunt then, too." I said, "I'm looking for a good field." He came back quickly, "Trust me, we'll find some birds. Come go with us." I said, "I'll let you know something in a few days."

I called Bob and told him how things had gone. Bob said, "You need to go. That trap shooting guy is coming down!" I didn't have much faith, since they didn't even have a dove field. I told Bob that I would give it several days, then call and confirm a hunt.

After a few days, I called Mike and asked if he still thought they could find some birds. He said, "Don't worry, we'll find some birds to shoot." I asked where and what time he wanted to meet. He told me to meet them at 5:45 a.m. on a county road off Highway 49 in Leflore County. I said, "Looking forward to meeting you, and I'll see you there."

I called Bob and told him the details of the meet, adding that there had been no mention of the Iowa guy. Bob said, "Trust me, he's coming, and they will find him some birds!" I was still a bit skeptical, but it was on now. Bob put together a team of state and federal agents to be waiting in the area for me to call and let them know what was happening. I booked a hotel in Greenwood for the night before.

The night before opening day of dove season, I arrived in Greenwood and called Mike to confirm our meeting for the next morning. He said that they had found some birds and would see me in the morning. Still, no mention of this famous trap shooter! Oh, well!

It was a long night, as was usual before a first contact meeting with someone covertly, especially a duck hunter. I had worked ducks all over the state and could easily have checked someone in this group, as I had no idea who was coming. My appearance was quite a bit different, with longer hair and a heavy beard. My cover was that I owned a landscaping business.

When my alarm went off at 4:30 a.m., I felt like I had just gone to sleep. I grabbed a big cup of coffee and headed to our meeting spot, not knowing what was about to unfold. I arrived early, at 5:30 a.m., and couldn't believe it as I pulled in behind a vehicle on the side of the road with an Iowa license plate! I had a recorder in my shirt and, before opening the door, cut it on and prefaced it with date, time, and my name.

As I was getting out of my truck, a man got out of the other truck, and we introduced ourselves, shaking hands. It was Bart Sikes, and I thought to myself, "Bob was right!" The circumstances worked in my favor, but the mosquitoes were about to carry us off. I invited him to sit in my truck as we waited. We jumped into my truck and, oh, he was a talker! He started telling in detail about all the geese and other birds he had killed on his way south, giving numbers killed and places he hunted. Getting it all on tape, I almost hated to see the headlights that pulled up behind us.

It was the Steverson brothers. We all got out and spoke briefly, and they said to follow them. We then got into our respective vehicles. Another vehicle joined our group as we headed out. We all pulled off the road into a cotton field. Mike said there would be a lot of birds flying on the edge of the field, as we were between several large, prepared dove fields.

We set up along the edge of the field, and it was a very slow hunt. We could see quite a few doves, but most were flying far away from us. I shot one dove and saw Bart kill two that were retrieved and cripple another that he made no effort to retrieve. The Steverson brothers sat on each side of Bart and never fired a shot. The other person shot a few times, but I didn't see him kill anything. Things were not looking too good. About 8:30 a.m., we decided to call it done and head back. Mike said, "Follow me." The Steversons were definitely catering to Bart. They said, "Don't worry, we'll get into the birds this evening. We've got another spot!"

I followed them back to Mike's house, where I met two other individuals, Joe and David. Joe had been on the field with us earlier, but we had not met. We sat around and told hunting stories, as well as discussed prices on duck hunts. I heard one of the other guys tell Mike, "We can hunt that field this evening." Then Mike told the group of us, "We got a good field this afternoon. We'll head out there after lunch." Bart acted excited as he stated, "I've got plenty of shells!" We continued to listen, primarily to Bart. He loved to brag.

After lunch, we all headed to a field that was about ten miles from the house. This gave me time to contact Bob on my cell phone while I was driving and give him directions, so they could be nearby if needed. The field was a prepared dove field disked with sown wheat, alongside what appeared to be planted sunflowers that had been bushhogged on one side of the field. We all pulled off the road next to a fence, then exited our vehicles.

We looked at the field and all the doves on the nearby power lines. Joe said, looking at Mike, "I told you they weren't here." Mike said, "Where should we park?" I was getting the feeling that something was not right. Joe responded quietly, "They won't be back till next weekend." I acted as if I wasn't paying attention. Mike said, "We can park behind the trees in that hayfield across the fence; I know him."

I couldn't believe we were about to trespass with men who were running an outfitting operation. He never said we were trespassing, but it was very obvious because we were hiding the vehicles off the road! Joe said that he and David were going to come around through the woods on the other end of the field. They drove off, and the Steverson brothers, Bart, and I went into a hayfield at the other end of the disked field and parked our vehicles behind a small group of trees.

Mike told me to go to the center of the field where a small ditch divided the disked area from the sunflower field. He and his brother took Bart up on a small knoll where a point of trees stuck out in the field. As I was walking across the field, there were plenty of doves already flying. I positioned myself where I could observe Bart and the Steverson brothers on either side of him. Bart could shoot! He was steadily dropping birds, and the Steversons were his retrievers. I was trying to count his downed birds, but I could tell they were having trouble finding birds. The knoll where they were sitting had a lot of weeds, plus many of the doves he shot went down in the woods behind them.

I was continually shooting as the birds were pouring into the field. I had reached a limit but continued to just shoot as birds would fly past, getting up and walking to appear as if I were looking for downed doves. I would bend over with a dove in my hand, drop it, and pick it up, shaking it by its wing, then place it back in my vest.

When I knew that Bart had exceeded his limit, I squatted in the ditch and called Bob, advising of the count I had; I knew they had picked up a least twenty birds. Bob said, "Continue to hunt and see if they will let you go in the morning." Thinking we might be pushing it, I said, "I know he's got over the limit, and we're trespassing!" He said, "It will be better in the morning; maybe you can get a better count. I know they will go. You can do it!" I'm glad Bob had faith in me. Things were starting to slow down, and I started toward my truck.

As Bart and the Steversons approached, I was cleaning and bagging the last of my birds, acting as though I was hiding them in a little cooler in the cab of my truck. After closing the cooler, I put some clothing over it. As we were talking about the hunt, I elaborated on how I was looking forward to cooking those doves, also saying that I wished I had a few more. I asked Bart if he had much luck. He just laughed and said, "I killed a few." I asked if he liked to eat them. He said, "Not really, you want them?" I said, "Sure, I'd love to have them."

The Steverson brothers started counting birds; they made a pile of one limit (fifteen birds), then started another pile with only thirteen. Mike got a notepad from his truck; wrote the date, his hunting license number, and the words "fifteen doves"; and then signed it, saying, "Put this in the bag with the birds in case you get checked." John did the same with the other thirteen doves. They didn't invite me back, so I finally asked as everyone was starting to load up, "Y'all going in the morning?" Mike responded, "Yeah, you want to go?" I acted excited and said, "Man I would love to!" He said, "We'll meet back here little before daylight." I said, "I'll be here, can't wait! See y'all in the morning." We all shook hands and got into our vehicles, exiting the field.

I waited until I was several miles away before calling Bob. He was right again! I told him I would meet him at the hotel where I was staying and give him the doves and an update. Bob came to the hotel later and picked up the birds as we briefly discussed the activities of that day. He told me to call the following morning and let him know before the hunt was over, so they would know when to come in. They had driven by while we were hunting, so they knew the layout of the field.

I slept better but was a little excited as I knew things would be interesting the following morning. It didn't feel like I had shut my eyes when the alarm went off at 4:45 a.m. I grabbed a big cup of coffee at the local truck stop and hit the road, headed back to the field.

I was at the field when they showed up. I told Bart, "You need to get in the ditch with me; the birds were all over me yesterday!" The ground was disked along the ditch, and we could find his doves. He told the Steverson brothers that he was going to get in the ditch with me, and they went back on the knoll. The other hunters went back to the sunflower field where they had parked in the woods.

As the sun was beginning to brighten things up, doves were already coming in and landing in the field near us. Bart fired the first shot, dropping a dove, and things sped up as everyone started shooting. I was about seventy-five yards from Bart and could see everything he did. I didn't watch anyone else. It was difficult trying to shoot and keep up with his downed birds at the same time. The good thing was, there was no one close to us. He would pick up a dove every now and then, but he was consistently shooting them and making no effort to retrieve them.

I had reached the limit within the first hour of shooting and was getting concerned that Bart might notice that I wasn't killing any. Thankfully, he wasn't paying any attention to me. I knew he had dropped over thirty doves, so I walked down the ditch, as if I were looking for a downed dove. While in the ditch, I bent over and called Bob, saying, "He's well over the limit, y'all come in when the shooting slows down." Bob responded, "Okay."

I made my way back up the ditch to Bart, as the doves were beginning to slow down. Bart was still knocking the birds down, even as he was picking up a few walking in the field. I went to him and picked up several of his doves, carrying them to him. I told him, "Man, you sure can shoot!" He responded, "I love it!" He had made a pile with some of his doves in a wash that ran into the ditch away from where his stool and other gear were located.

As we continued to shoot, I saw a vehicle turn into the field. I kept on shooting. As I turned to Bart, he was headed to the truck. I almost laughed, saying, "Over your head!" He wasn't slowing down, but I did hear him say, "Feds!" I started walking up the ditch and could see officers coming out of the woods and getting out of the truck; one was headed toward me. He asked for my license and was checking the plug in my gun. He asked, "Where are your birds?"

By this time, I could tell that everyone had been contacted and Bob was with Bart near the truck. As I was walking to where my stool was, I whispered to the agent nonchalantly, "All the birds on the ground around us are Bart's, and he has some in the wash we are about to walk by; look to my left." The federal agent continued on with me and counted my doves. He then asked me to get my gear and follow him. He still had my hunting license and driver's license.

After we got to the truck, they separated us and interviewed everyone separately. State and federal agents were walking around Bart's gear, picking up doves. They piled them close to his other pile and took photographs. Bob escorted Bart out to where the doves and gear were located. After they returned, Bart was crying like a child. They took information from all of us on the field, confiscating all the doves, and also seized Bart's gun. Bob explained the violations and federal laws concerning each, then told us all they would be in contact with us. They then left the field.

I acted as if that was the first time I had been checked, but also tried to act a little angry. The Steversons weren't too concerned with me and the others as they tried to comfort Bart. It was almost comical. I told Mike, as I was putting my gear in the truck, "I'm gonna still call you about a duck hunt." He commented, "Don't worry about those feds, holler at me later!" I shook hands with everyone and left.

Following the covert hunt, agents interviewed Bart and the others several times, with the subjects' attorneys present. It was finally divulged that I was an undercover agent. Bart confessed to numerous federal violations of the Migratory Bird Treaty Act in several states. Bob let him think that the Fish and Wildlife Service had agents following him and documenting what he had done in other states, using information I had recorded from Bart's stories the first day we met. Oh, what a talker he was, and very good with details!

They all pleaded guilty to numerous federal violations. Bart's gun became the property of the government. He lost his hunting privileges in the United States for three years and paid several thousand dollars in fines. The Steverson brothers were also charged with aiding and abetting, losing their hunting privileges for three years and paying a hefty fine.

As with many cases I worked, it took the initiative of Agent Oliveri and then the follow-up of many state and federal agents, to bring it all together in the end with an enthusiastic assistant US attorney, John Dowdy. I owe a lot in my career to both Bob and John, for knowledge of the law and of what's needed to win a case. We never lost a case!

CHAPTER 25

OPERATION STONED DUCK, MY LAST OP

After Operation Rooster (chapter 20), I received information through one of the subjects I interviewed that a guy named John wanted to talk to me. John was a local whose name had come up many times during conversations at Eddie's place. It was evident that he might be a prime target. What we didn't know was that he actually thought we had a warrant for him, and he wanted to work out a deal. We had nothing, but what the heck, we didn't have to tell him.

I gave John a call and set up a meeting at a hotel in another town. John showed up on time and, oh, what a wealth of information he had! He knew of law enforcement officers involved in narcotics, insurance fraud (by farmers), theft involving farm equipment and cotton, theft involving farm-raised catfish, trophy-deer headlighting, and waterfowl baiting. I was overwhelmed! If just part of what he had told me was true, oh my!

John was sharp as a tack; he was spouting out names and addresses faster than I could write them down. The only bad thing was, he cussed like a sailor and it got to me. I told him we would get together in a few days and ride around. I wanted him to show me some of the areas and discuss in more detail what he had told me about. He agreed.

The next meeting with John, I took Agent Greg Johnson with me. Greg and I picked John up at his home, and he started taking us around, showing and telling us what and who he knew and what they were doing. I told him we were recording everything instead of just taking notes to make sure we got it all. John could not make a sentence without starting it, "That G#% d*#%)* m#@#$# f**)&##!" After a couple of hours of his filthy mouth, I said "Let's call it a day!" We took him home; Greg pulled up to John's house, and we told him we would get back with him as he got out of the vehicle.

I had been struggling to just sit there and not say something about the way he talked. I was afraid to say too much, because this guy could really put us onto some stuff! Greg could tell something was bothering me. As he started to pull away, I told him, "Wait a minute, stop and let me out." I hollered at John as he was entering his home, "Hey, we need to talk just a minute." John had a look of confusion, as did Greg, wondering why I'd gotten out.

I approached John in his front yard and said, "I don't know you very well and I don't want to jeopardize what you might be able to help us with, but I'm a Christian and I would prefer if you wouldn't use my Heavenly Father's name in vain when you are with me." John just looked down and said, "I know I shouldn't do that." I said, "Do you know Jesus?" He said, still looking down, "Yes." I said, "Why don't we start this thing over?" He looked at me kind of confused. I said, "Can I pray with you?" He said, "Please!"

I put my hand on that big, rough fellow and started praying, asking God to be with us and to help John with his life, as well as his family. Greg had to be wondering what was going on. When we finished praying, this big, rough and tough fellow was wiping tears from his eyes, as was I. We shook hands, and I headed back to the truck. Greg did not say anything for several miles down the road, nor did I. He finally said, "What happened back there?" I told him, and he said, "I was wondering if y'all were praying or something." Then we laughed.

The following week, we met with John again and rode with him for about four hours. It was like riding with a different man. I guess he didn't feel intimidated or nervous, as only a couple of times did he use profanity, and on those occasions, he apologized. Over the next several months, John's information started coming together; he was introducing us to individuals he had spoken about, and so far it appeared that he was right about everything he had told us.

I was the supervisor of special operations and was planning Operation Stoned Duck to be my last, as I had been working covertly for almost fifteen years and was getting burned out. We had given the case that name because there were narcotics and ducks involved. Agents Johnson, Reese, and Wilkins would be the primary covert agents, and I was going to play a role as the cautious buyer. Agents went on a couple of teal hunts in some baited areas to open the case. It wasn't much, but through the covert hunts we could see that things were happening just as John had said. Several individuals would come up from the Mississippi Gulf Coast and stay at local hotels or camps. They were very boastful, while under the influence of alcohol and drugs, about how they were shooting trophy deer at night along the Mississippi River.

Due to the investigation, we decided to place a house trailer in the area where most of the illegal activity was taking place. This was where I lived and

Poaching started early with this crew as their antlers were still in velvet. (Photo courtesy of the MDWFP.)

where the other coverts agents allegedly sold their deer and slept when in the area hunting. It was just a ruse to make them appear to be violators. John was coming through quite well, and we had become very good friends, due the amount of time we had been spending together. He was always asking about the Lord and telling me about his family. He was living with a young lady and his son from a previous marriage. He said that his son was a good boy and that he did not want him to turn out like his daddy. John was probably one of the most skilled hunters and poachers I had ever met. He had been using cocaine but said he quit because of his son.

It was October. A group of guys John had told us about, and introduced agents to during the teal hunts, were in the area. They said they were bowhunting on the wildlife management areas along the river. John said they were headlighting. We invited them over to the trailer as we cooked some fish. Two of them showed, both young fellows in their early twenties, and were running their mouths due to the quantity of drugs (crack) and beer they had consumed during the evening. Everything was being recorded, as the trailer was wired with video and audio equipment.

Greg and Jerry (Agent Reese) asked if they had killed anything yet. They laughed and said they'd only killed one deer the night before but were planning

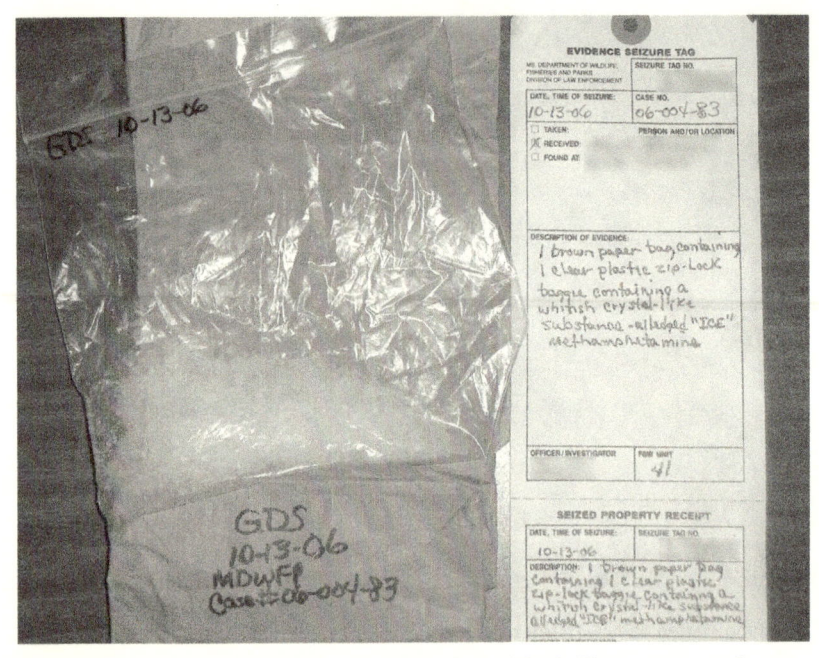

Meth "ice" that was purchased during Operation Stoned Duck. (Photo courtesy of the MDWFP.)

on going again that night. Greg asked if we could go along, as we needed some meat. I played the cautious guy, warning, "I don't want no trouble with the law!" Greg offered to take his truck; it was wired with video and audio in the cab and toolbox. They left the trailer around 9:30 p.m. and returned around 1:00 a.m. with two nice bucks they'd killed and a wild hog that John had shot. Things went well, and they told us they would see us again the following week. They also said that Blake, our primary target, would be up the following week. Blake was also supposed to be moving large amounts of drugs.

The following week, Blake showed up and fell right in with the group. They headlighted five deer, all trophy bucks, and even posed with the deer they were shooting as agents took photos. Blake was very boastful about all the deer he had illegally killed and had little concern about game wardens or the law.

Over the next several months, we documented evidence as they shot twenty-plus deer by illegal means and sold narcotics (meth/ice and marijuana) on multiple occasions. Blake and the agents were getting along well, and the case was progressing rapidly. Several local poachers had also gotten involved, as they thought we were poachers, and even asked if we could store a couple of illegal deer for them. Blake had invited agents to his place on the coast the next

Marijuana was also purchased during this operation. (Photo courtesy of the MDWFP.)

time they were down. The undercover work couldn't get any better! We were slowly working John out of the equation.

An issue that came up during visits to the coast was that the targets had been poaching deer on the grounds of the Stennis Space Center, a secure federal facility that opened in the 1960s during NASA's Apollo program and was used for testing rocket engines. One of the agents was able to get a picture of a mounted deer at Blake's house that had a stolen federal sign on the bottom of the mount. Several of the guards were friends with the targets and, when they saw a big buck, would contact Blake or one of the others. Our targets would kill it, giving the guards some of the meat.

I contacted John Dowdy, the assistant US attorney handling the case, and advised him of the new developments involving the rocket engine testing area. John was concerned and wanted to involve the FBI, as the facility was federal property. Boy, did that open a can of worms. The FBI assigned Special

Agent Joe Nelson to the case. I met with him and John to discuss what we had uncovered. At first, he didn't seem too happy that he was going to be working with "game wardens." After he had been briefed on the case, he seemed a little more enthusiastic. Then he told John that anyone involved covertly would have to be psychologically evaluated. I thought, "You have got to be kidding!"

I had been working covertly for close to fifteen years. But all covert agents involved had to undergo a psychological evaluation before we could continue with anything the FBI would be investigating. When I told the guys, they all laughed at first. I said, "What the heck? I knew we were a little crazy, now I guess we will find out!" The FBI was going to fly us all to Washington, DC. I had never been to DC before so thought it might be interesting.

We arrived in DC a couple of weeks later. We each had to take a test on a computer that took several hours. We found out that folks up there were not very hospitable. The ladies who were giving us our written test couldn't understand that we would always respond "yes ma'am" or "no ma'am" when we were asked something. I finally told them that most men raised in the South always responded that way. They were amazed.

After the written test, we each had to talk with a psychiatrist. All of my men went through before me. I guess I was last since I was the supervisor. I was a little nervous, as, when I sat down, I saw that the psychiatrist had notes from each of the agents before me. He sat there just looking at me, bouncing his pen on the pad, almost as if he was angry.

His first statement was, "Your men said y'all pray together sometimes." I didn't quite know where he was going but said, "Yes we do." He said, "About what?" I responded, "We are under a lot of pressure and gone from home a lot; we are a very tight-knit group, as we can't discuss things with other officers or coworkers. We don't socialize with anyone in law enforcement outside our special ops group." I said, "When my guys are having problems, we pray together. I tell them if things aren't good at home, they don't need to be working covert."

He just sat there and then said, "Do you not have a problem with working undercover and being a Christian?" I said, "Yes, a little. I feel guilty sometimes, because I sometimes get close to the people that I'm working and feel like I have betrayed them. Then I think about what they're doing or have done and know that this is the only way to catch them. I'm just doing my job. I pray about it and move on."

He sat there with a puzzled look on his face. He then said, "You know, the men in our office email each other; we don't even talk unless we pass each other in the hall." I know I probably looked dumbfounded, because I was thinking, "Maybe I need to be counseling you!" After a brief pause, he said, "I don't have anything further; go down to the next office and he will go over your test."

"Thank you," I said, and headed down the hall to my next evaluation, not sure what had just happened in there.

I could see the other guys down the hall, looking at me with smirky grins. As I entered the next office, I could see red circles on several of the pages. The evaluator's first question was, "Have you ever thought about killing someone?" I said, "I'm in law enforcement; yes, I've had to draw my weapon before when I was in uniform. Sure, I've thought about it." He kind of laughed, asked a few more insignificant questions, and said, "You and your guys did fine." Still chuckling, he said, "Thanks for being honest." I was a little puzzled. We all passed, whatever that meant, but I knew one thing: I was ready to go back to Mississippi!

Back at home, the investigation was progressing. While the agents were working with Blake on the Gulf Coast, they gathered information that one of our own (a game warden) was a good friend of Blake's group, and he supposedly knew all about what they did. That was not something I wanted to hear; not only what he knew about, but also what they said he'd done was very disheartening. They claimed that he was careless about shooting over the limit of ducks. I didn't want to believe what I was hearing on the taped conversation. I felt sick to my stomach! I did not want anything to do with investigating a game warden, but I told the guys that we would continue the case, and, if he turned up and was actually doing what they said, he would be prosecuted with the rest of them. The one they were speaking of, I had actually worked with many years earlier on the coast. He was a great guy and hilarious to be around. I couldn't believe what they were saying, or just didn't want to believe.

It was getting close to teal season when we got information that our game warden, Willard, was planning a hunt with his buddies in the Mississippi Delta. We were able to find out where and to check the place before they hunted. There was bait everywhere! We photographed the bait and took samples for evidence. After consulting with John Dowdy, we decided to do surveillance and document the hunt. We had several agents set up at strategic locations around the old catfish pond to video and count teal as they were shot and picked up. No contact was to be made. Willard showed up and did just what they said he would do. He and the other hunters shot over the limit, standing in bait that was visible everywhere. I didn't like it, but it was true. It was all documented and filed in a report. I hated it, but he was not above the law just because he wore that uniform. In fact, it made me angry because he was making all the good wardens look bad.

Finally, as with all covert cases, it was time to close. Another two years of investigation had documented numerous individuals violating both state and federal game laws, selling narcotics, and engaging in security violations at a

Illegal waterfowl taken during the investigation (teal and wood ducks; violations: over limit, closed season, and over bait). (Photo courtesy of the MDWFP.)

government complex (misdemeanor and felony violations). We were all ready to close the investigation!

But we had one more issue. The group of poachers was planning a big dove hunt, and two of our covert agents were invited to the hunt. They had even been at Blake's home the week before the season and documented them baiting the field, using birdseed and wheat. We got evidence—photographs of fifty-pound bags of birdseed and wheat under Blake's carport.

It was decided after discussion with US Fish and Wildlife Special Agent Robert Oliveri (Bob) and John Dowdy that we would bust the baited dove field on opening weekend of dove season. Then we would get warrants and close the investigation. Bob put together a team of federal agents, and I picked four state officers. None of the officers or agents had any idea where we were going until the night before, when we met at a hotel near Hattiesburg, Mississippi. We had a briefing in one of the hotel rooms and discussed the details of what would be going down, and that there would be two undercover agents on the field. The officers were to take information from the undercover agents just like any other hunters on the field.

At 3:30 a.m. the following morning, we headed out to set up on the field before daylight. The plan was to observe the hunt and document any over limits until it was about over. Then Bob would give the signal to enter the field over the radio. I would be hidden close to a house in the woods to do surveillance on anyone coming and going. Just before daylight, several vehicles pulled up to Blake's house, and hunters were walking across the field setting up to hunt. As the sun rose and the sky started to lighten up, doves began pouring into the baited field. The shooting was steady for a couple of hours.

About 8:30 a.m., I noticed a green truck drive past the house onto the field. It was an MDWFP truck with two wardens, one being Willard, whom we had observed earlier. I radioed Bob and said, "Willard and another warden are on the field." He quickly responded, "I see them, we'll just see what they do; everyone just stay put till they leave!" Willard and the other warden walked around the field checking licenses, but not counting birds. After about thirty minutes, they got back in their truck and left the field. The doves had about quit flying, and it appeared that most of the hunters were starting to get ready to leave the field. Bob radioed, "Everyone hit the field." I continued to just do surveillance, as I didn't want to be spotted by anyone.

Two federal agents in a vehicle met Willard and the other warden on the road leaving the house. They continued onto the field (later, they said that Willard looked at them as their vehicle passed and, knowing who they were, continued to drive away). A routine bust was done and each hunter was interviewed, bait was photographed (samples taken), personal information was taken, and each was told they would be contacted by the US attorney's office concerning their violations of hunting over a baited dove field and killing over the limit. All the doves were seized, as they had been killed illegally.

Blake and his little band of poachers were ready to start killing deer by September. We tried to put them off as much as possible, but they were going with or without us. We documented as many game violations as possible, along with making several more narcotics purchases. We were able to document some of the poaching and trespassing activity at the Stennis Space Center, as Agent Reese was able to go with them on one hunt. He documented the security guard calling, and where and how Blake and his buddies were entering through a hole cut in the fence in an area without surveillance cameras.

Now we were really ready to close the operation. We worked on arrest warrants and search warrants for several weeks until we got everything in order. We decided, due to Blake's earlier comments about law enforcement, that we needed to get him in an open area to execute arrest warrants. Greg and I were going to give him a call and stop by to get him outside, at which time the arrest team would execute the arrest warrant for sale of narcotics and a search warrant on his home.

Greg and I were within a few miles of his residence when we made the call. Blake answered and was at home. Greg told him we were in the area and wanted

These mounted deer and firearms were confiscated during the execution of search warrants after arrest. (Photo courtesy of the MDWFP.)

to stop by. He said sure, stop by. I was wearing a wire and gave the arrest team the signal to come in. I had used this method many times in my career, and it always seemed like time then went into slow motion, waiting on that first vehicle to pull in. Everything went smoothly, and it almost seemed like Blake was expecting it. He was handcuffed and placed in the back seat of one of the federal agents' vehicles for transport.

Bob gave the signal over the radio for all the arrest teams to serve warrants (search and arrest). Over one hundred guns, close to one hundred mounted heads, photographs, computers, and narcotics were seized that day.

We made many felony arrests over the next several months, with follow-up interviews. Since this was my last investigation, I helped Joe (FBI) and Bob (US Fish and Wildlife Service) with the interviews.

I had visited jails across many states throughout my career in law enforcement, and never were they places that I cared to go. A jail was a cold, solemn locale, one that generally didn't hold many smiles, as men's and women's lives were at a crossroads. The county jail in central Mississippi held one of the many individuals we'd recently arrested.

Agent Joe Nelson and I turned our firearms over to the jailer after showing our law enforcement identification. We were requesting a visit with Scott Jones,

More firearms and mounted deer confiscated during the execution of our search warrants. (Photo courtesy of the MDWFP.)

one of the subjects awaiting trial since the close of Operation Stoned Duck. Scott was facing charges of sale of narcotics (marijuana and crystal meth) and numerous state and federal wildlife violations.

A metal clank followed a loud buzz as the jailer opened an electronic door, allowing us to enter the secure area. Looking down the hall to the left, we could see hands hanging out of small openings in the doors to individual cells. The jailer interrupted mumbled conversation as he spoke in a stern voice, telling Scott, "Get up, you have some visitors." I watched as the once towering figure of a man now slumped as he stepped backward out of his cell to the waiting jailer. A deputy assisted with placing him in ankle shackles and cuffing his hands to his waist. They escorted him to room #2, exited, and told us, "He's yours, holler when you're through and we'll come get him." As Agent Nelson nodded to the jailers, I said, "Let's do it." Pulling the large metal door closed behind us, we stood briefly making small talk with little or no response from Scott. It was evident he wanted to talk, by the way his eyes were fixed on me with both fear and hate.

Scott was only twenty-one years old and facing twenty-plus years in the federal penitentiary for the sale of narcotics and numerous wildlife violations. He had older friends who'd led him in the wrong direction of drug trafficking and other illegal activity. He thought they had it all and wanted to be like them. He got his wish, as they were also incarcerated pending federal prosecution for drug, wildlife, and other miscellaneous charges. The eight other individuals had actually been primary targets of the covert investigation, while Scott was one who got picked up along the course of the investigation. We had spoken with Scott several times prior, setting up a plea agreement through his attorney and the US attorney.

The interrogation room had bluish-gray concrete walls and a floor that was probably the same color at one time, but was now overlaid with black through out due to all the scuff marks from prisoners and jailers. It had only one door with a small window, a table bolted to the floor, four old metal chairs, and a camera mounted in the upper left-hand corner.

The mood was cold as we started the interview, easing into the conversation by asking questions for which we already knew the answers. This would be the last time we'd speak with Scott. We were trying to get the name of an individual who had been with him at one of the drug transactions during which covert investigators were the purchasers, but Scott wouldn't give it up. He talked around, but it was nothing worth wasting our time over.

At the close of the interview, I told Scott that I would pray for him. Scott didn't respond verbally, just gave a look that would kill. Joe and I left the interview room and notified the jailers that we were through with Scott, so they could take the prisoner back to his cell.

Scott and I would see each other again a few weeks later in federal court, as he faced the consequences of his actions over the prior few years. As people were filing into the courtroom, the prosecuting attorney and agents involved, as well as the families and friends of those facing the judge on that day, whispered among themselves. Each time the large wooden doors of the courtroom opened, people would turn and look at those entering. Scott's mother and father made their way to a seat; I looked a second time back at the door as Scott's grandmother stood at the back of the courtroom, and when our eyes met, she made her way toward me.

We had met the day he was arrested, while I was serving the search warrant at his residence, and we talked a bit that day. I told Scott's mother and grandmother, as they were both very upset, that I would pray for them and hoped everything would get better. Everyone in the courtroom was watching as the little lady approached me. I stood, as she appeared to want to speak. As I bent down, she whispered quietly, "Thank you." She then made her way to the rest of the family and took a seat as people looked on, puzzled about what had just taken place. I was confused but said a silent prayer, asking God to help the family.

The courtroom quieted, other than the sniffles from loved ones crying, as Scott, handcuffed, shackled, and wearing his orange jumpsuit, was escorted in by two US Marshals and pointed to his seat next to his attorney. The once towering, six-foot-two, two-hundred-pound, proud young man looked like a withered old man who had nothing to live for. He slowly turned and stared at me, before looking back at his family and their pain. It was evident that he was scared as he fought back tears, not knowing what was about to take place in the next minutes and years to come.

"All rise!" spoke the bailiff, as the federal judge entered and took his prestigious position above everyone else in the room. He read all the routine legal entries to begin court proceedings. Since Scott was entering a plea of guilty and all the details had been settled prior to court, everything flowed smoothly as Assistant US Attorney Dowdy reviewed the charges against Scott. The judge offered Scott's defense the opportunity to correct or challenge. He did not. The judge asked Scott to stand as he read the charges against him and went forward with sentencing. Scott's mother was crying as that was completed. Scott hugged his family and was escorted from the courtroom, to spend the next four years of his life in the federal penitentiary system. Scott's road in life was taking a turn, as was mine. That was my last case before retirement. Neither of us knew that our paths would cross again through God's plans.

I retired after Operation Stoned Duck was completely closed. I started a nuisance animal control business and went back to my dream of trapping. Four years after my retirement, I was teaching at the Mississippi Trappers Association's Trapper's College, an annual event to promote trapping and educate people who were interested.

The first day of this class, I looked across the crowd, and standing in the corner was Scott. My first thought as I saw him staring at me was, "This might not be good!" I told one of the instructors to keep an eye on him. Nothing happened until that night, when a small group was talking about plans for the following day. I knew that Scott was standing close to me, but I had not acknowledged him. David, one of the instructors, introduced himself to Scott and then told Scott who I was. Scott shook my hand and told David, "We know each other." I could tell by his demeanor that he had no ill feelings toward me. We talked in the group, but nothing was brought up of how we knew each other.

Over the next three days, Scott and I spent quite a bit of time together. He had a job working for a landowner as a caretaker in southern Mississippi. He was at Trapper's College to learn how to trap coyotes and hogs. We talked a little about the past, but primarily about the future. By the end of Trapper's College, we had developed a good relationship. I gave him my phone number and told him to give me a call if he had any questions concerning trapping.

Over the next year, Scott called several times, primarily telling me what critters he had caught and also that he had gotten married and was expecting a child. During the months to follow, I could tell by our phone conversations that he wanted to tell me something, but just wouldn't open up. He finally called and asked if he could meet with me. I put him off for a while. I wasn't sure if that would be very smart. He continued to call and told me, "I need to talk to someone I can trust!" So I told him that I would meet with him at the First Baptist Church of Fannin at 9:00 a.m. that Sunday. I said, "I teach Sunday School; you come to class, we'll go to church, then after church we can grab something to eat and talk." He got quiet for a moment and said, "I'll be there." I told my wife I wasn't sure whether he would show or not.

That Sunday morning, I saw Scott pull into the parking lot alone. My wife and I greeted him in the parking lot, and we entered the church together. He went to Sunday School and then sat in church with Betty and I. I could tell he seemed uncomfortable, but when Brother Ron finished his sermon and did the invitation, Scott stood and headed to the altar. Betty and I followed him down to the altar. He got on his knees and was praying. I got on one side of him and Betty on the other, and we all prayed together. He was crying and sweating profusely as we prayed. It was a moment I'll never forget.

After church, Scott and I went to a little café for lunch. He told me, "They are trying to get me back involved with drugs and stuff at home. I don't know what to do!" I said, "You have got to get away from them, or you will wind up back in prison! I'll try to help you find a job if you get away from there." He wasn't sure if his wife would move, and she was pregnant. Over the next couple of months, he got an apartment and continued to come to church and Sunday School. I had a friend who was a taxidermist and needed some help. Scott had an interest in taxidermy and loved the work. As it turned out, John Dowdy, the prosecutor of Scott's cases, had a son who was also working at the taxidermist's. Scott found a little house to rent and got his wife and son moved. He had started another chapter in his life, and we had become not only friends but brothers in Christ!

We were having a wild game supper at the church, and I was in charge of getting the guest speaker. I asked Scott if he would give his testimony. He said, "I have never spoke before!" I told him I would help him get it together, so he agreed. We met and prayed for the next several weeks.

The night of the supper, Scott was nervous, but God gave him the words to tell his story. It was awesome! No one knew his past, though he had been coming to church and gotten to know quite a few people. He got a standing ovation from the crowd, which included his wife, son, mother, father, and grandmother. What a moment! God is good!

Scott and I have been able to speak at many churches together since and tell our story. He now owns his own taxidermy business; God has truly blessed his life!

I also kept in touch with John, stopping by or by phone. I stayed on him that he needed to marry his girlfriend and not just be living with her. He said, "I keep asking, but she won't!" He said, "I think she doesn't trust me because my son thinks I'm doing bad things still, you know, since I hang around you." He asked, "Since it's over, could you tell him that I'm not bad?" I told him I would see him in a couple of days. I showed up at his house a little after 5:00 p.m. one afternoon and told him I would tell his son.

John and I went into his house and waited for his son to get home from school. When John's son entered the house, he just gave me a bad look and headed to his room. His daddy told him to come in there with us. When James (his son) came in the room, I stood up, stuck out my hand, and introduced myself as Agent Prince, also showing him my badge and identification. I said, "I'm over the special operations for the Mississippi Department of Wildlife, Fisheries, and Parks, and your daddy has been helping us apprehend some tough violators the past few years." James's face lit up and he hugged his daddy; John was in tears when his girlfriend came in and, yeah, I told her, too. I thanked him and told him if there was anything I could ever do for him, to not hesitate to call. We shook hands, and I left.

John gave me a call about a week later and said, "Guess what, I'm getting married!" We laughed and joked a bit, and I congratulated him. He kept me informed of his son going to school and getting caught up in sports, as well as he and his wife being involved in their local church. We don't know the final outcome in anything we do, but God always has a plan if we'll just put Him first! God is good!

State award for covert investigations.

International award for covert investigations given to our special operations unit by the International Association of Fish and Wildlife Agencies. (Left to right: Kennie Prince, Glen Jackson, Colonel Curtis Green, Lieutenant Colonel John Collins, Gary Smith, and Dustin Blount.)

AUTHOR'S NOTE

I am a Christian, having accepted Jesus Christ as my Lord and Savior when I was eighteen years old. Even though I had been raised in a good Christian home and knew the Lord, my Christian walk was not very recognizable. I went to church periodically and, although I was saved, I was not the type of Christian that had a glow about him, and my fruit was light. I, like many other Christians, was "undercover." Going to church every now and then, the rest of the week I sank back into my covert position of the World, using profanity and having immoral conversations when around "the guys."

My supervisor in special operations, Greg Waggoner, is a Christian and actually *lives what he believes!* Although he didn't always know it, he has been a great mentor and friend. Greg doesn't say much about his faith unless asked, though his light is always shining. During my time as a covert agent, the Lord worked in ways that would further open my eyes to Christ and what being a Christian was truly about, even while living a life in the underworld.

I have been blessed with a wonderful family. My wife, Betty, and I were introduced through mutual friends, each of us having been divorced. We both had children. She had two sons, Michael and Glenn, and I had a son and a daughter, Cody and Jennifer. Today's statistics show that such a relationship has very little chance of survival, with 70 percent ending in divorce. We have now been married for twenty-five years, and until death do we part.

We each vowed to put God first, then each other, with the children to follow, treating each as them as our own flesh and blood. Michael and Glenn lived with us, and Jennifer and Cody visited every other weekend. God was blessing our broken lives, even though it didn't always appear that way! Satan throws all kinds of obstacles into our lives; thank God that, when we turn to Him, He will pick us up and use it for His glory. "We" now have four children and six grandchildren whom we each call our own and love as our own.

Throughout life, everyone goes through those valleys when everything seems to be unraveling with no way to stop it! Psalms 23:4, "Even though I walk through the valley of the shadow of death, I fear no evil, for You are with me; Your rod and Your staff, they comfort me." Thank God for the valleys!

Jennifer and Cody asked to come live with Betty and me. A "nasty" custody battle was on the horizon. During this "valley" involving family, I asked everyone for advice, even the pastor! Yes, I actually went to the preacher seeking an answer, and, though he didn't give an answer, he did give advice. He prayed with me and told me to continue to pray. I didn't follow the advice until all other sources had been exhausted. No one had an answer that seemed right to me. God knew what was right, though, and He was going to make it happen.

My life looked as though it was about to fall apart while I watched, with no way to stop it from happening. Finally, as so many Christians do, I turned to Christ as my last resort and pleaded for guidance and help. I did this on my knees in front of my home while cutting grass one day. As I cried out to God begging for answers; tears flowed from my face, like a small child sobbing. I knew I wasn't supposed to barter with God, but I told God of all the things I would stop doing or that I would do! I cried to God, "Just tell me what to do and I'll go to church and do anything!"

I was so weak I couldn't get up as my wife pulled into the drive. She helped me up and to the front porch to sit in the swing, trying to get me to pull myself together before the kids got home. I told her what I had been asking of God and also what I had been promising. She tried to comfort me, but I needed an answer from God!

My mother's car pulled into the drive, bringing Jennifer and Cody home from school. Normally they would have just gone into the house and started on their evening snacks. Jennifer did, but Cody came to the front porch where Betty and I were sitting in the swing. He was only eight years old and had no idea what was happening. He approached us and, looking up at me, said, "Don't worry, Daddy, everything is going to be OK," laying his head against me. I fought back tears as God answered my prayer through the words of my son. The next several months were extremely painful for all involved. We were able to obtain custody without ever going into the courtroom.

Like many other Christians, we were going to church again and even to Sunday School, for the moment! Kind of holding up my end of what I had promised God? I didn't quite know where God was about to take me. After church one Sunday, the pastor asked if I was going to be at a prayer meeting that Wednesday. I said, "Sure, Preacher!" The preacher then stated that he was not going to be there and asked if would I lead prayer meeting. I stuttered before the answer slowly came out: "I guess." Never having led a prayer service, I was scared to death.

God had answered my prayers, and over the next few months, my life was slowly put back together, better than ever. I read God's word and prayed diligently. My faith grew daily as I could see God working in my life. I was actually growing in Christ! I started understanding what I had heard preached so many times: you can't have much of a relationship with someone you don't talk with or get to know through prayer and reading HIS WORD.

I was asked to help teach Sunday School. That was one of the hardest decisions I ever made; I was scared. It wasn't fear of speaking in front of people, having taught at the law enforcement academy and given numerous talks concerning wildlife law enforcement, as I had some experience with that. It was the fear of speaking about God's holy word. James 3 tells us that ministers and teachers will be judged more harshly than others. So does 1 Timothy 3:1, which states, "Not many of you should become teachers, my fellow believers, because you know that we who teach will be judged more strictly." I read God's word concerning teaching and was unsure whether I should, considering my past. I tried substituting for a while and before long had my own class. God had given me the "gift" to speak; therefore, God was opening doors. Maybe my lack of seeking God's will was why I never saw the opened doors. Other doors were opened, such as mission trips, becoming a deacon, and being placed on several committees within the church.

One of the church committees that I was placed on was the Constitution and Bylaws Committee. Didn't seem like much, other than reading over the constitution periodically and maybe changing a few words as the "little country church" was starting to grow. After a few years of being on the committee, I was elected chairman. I think I got the position during the meeting I missed. No one wanted that job!!!

Our church was between pastors, and the search committee was working hard trying to find the pastor whom God wanted to serve in our church. It was also time to update the church constitution. There was a retired pastor who had been preaching some, and he offered to help with the constitution. I welcomed his help.

During one of the meetings, the pastor made numerous changes concerning scripture that would reference the qualifications of a pastor. The pastor was making a reference to "a husband of but one wife." He then used a different scripture to describe the position of a deacon. 1 Timothy 3:8 states, "In the same way, deacons are to be worthy of respect, sincere, not indulging in much wine, and not pursuing dishonest gain." 1 Timothy 3:10 states, "They must first be tested; and then let them serve as deacons if they are beyond reproach." I also know that 1 Timothy 1:15 states, "Here is a trustworthy saying that deserves full acceptance: Christ Jesus came into the world to save sinners, among of whom I am the worst." I (cautiously) asked why he had done that, as I thought the same scripture applied to both. No one in the room commented as I made that point and asked those on the committee to respond. No one did; everyone seemed to just stare.

I then asked the pastor, "If a man had been married five times and came to know the Lord, were his sins forgiven? If he felt led to preach the word and serve in that manner, should he not be able to?" The pastor didn't say much, as I made it very clear that the constitution would go with God's word. I asked if the scripture applies to pastors, deacons, teachers, and elders. He dodged the answer. I knew that he knew I had been divorced, so I went ahead and stated it for anyone who may have not known. I said that I would gladly step down from my position if we all agreed.

My position was that if it applied to the pastor, then it should apply to each position within the church (1 Timothy 3:1–13). The pastor laid the constitution on the table (frustrated) and stated that the committee did not need his help any further. Within a month, the church had a new pastor, and, without a doubt, he was a Godsend.

I was still working as a covert agent during my growth as a Christian and even questioned what I did, as to whether it was right. For example, winning people's confidence only to betray them later, with the end result being the incarceration of individuals, many of whom I had actually become friends with! I struggled with it, discussed it with the preacher, but continued to work undercover. I did do things a lot differently, for instance in the way I talked. God protected me, as He had plans even in the "dark" covert world in which I was involved. God showed me that no matter where I was, He was with me!

ACKNOWLEDGMENTS

I couldn't mention all who played a role in the advancement of my career; it is a long list.

But the most important has been God, having filled the most important role in every step of my life and career. I thank the Lord for being the guiding light that was always before me. I have been blessed with a father and mother who were great examples and mentors. I am especially blessed with my wife Betty, who puts up with me and has helped me through some very tough times. She is a Godsend. God blessed us with four children: Michael, Glenn, Jennifer, and Cody. We now have six grandchildren. I'm proud to say that our oldest sons, Michael and Glenn, are both in law enforcement and have made great careers in it. Our youngest son, Cody, is full-time military with the National Guard's special forces. Our daughter, Jennifer, works at a resort in Saint Thomas. We live as Joshua 24:15 states: "But as for me and my house, we will serve the Lord."

I am also especially appreciative of all the game wardens, biologists, US Fish and Wildlife Service agents, US attorneys, and other people across the country who sacrifice so much for wildlife conservation. A special thank you goes to the men and women of law enforcement, firefighters, first responders, and the military who sacrifice so much for us daily! God bless you!

God is good!

ABOUT THE AUTHOR

Photo by Jennifer Rutledge

Condy (Kennie) Prince III grew up in Brandon, Mississippi. He was blessed to have been raised by Christian parents who enjoyed all of God's creation and brought their children up enjoying it also.

He started hunting with his father, who had to carry Kennie on his back many times. You see, Kennie was crippled with Legg-Perthes disease as a child through his elementary years. One of the many obstacles that the Lord has brought him through.

Kennie's grandfather Prince ran a bait shop where he worked after school and got to interact with fishermen, hunters, game wardens, and one man who was a trapper.

That trapper gave Kennie a couple of old traps and showed him how to set them while at the store. Kennie was amazed with the traps. He caught his first beaver in 1968 and has trapped ever since. His father was a great encourager and purchased him traps, along with some books about trapping. His father believed in working hard and was a great example for him. Kennie always worked and trapped for extra income.

During college, he guided on a ranch in Colorado in the fall. After graduating from college, he started a career with Mississippi Game and Fish (now the Mississippi Department of Wildlife, Fisheries, and Parks) and became a game warden. God opened many doors for him through that agency, and he met many lifelong friends along the way.

Kennie accepted Christ at the age of eighteen but got off track with God's purpose for him for a while. Thankfully, he got back on track.

Since his retirement from law enforcement, Kennie traps nuisance animals for a living such as beavers, hogs, coyotes, and alligators. He's definitely in his element there!

He loves telling about how God has changed his life at many speaking events. I guess if you're reading this, you'll know that he has taken up writing as well.

Kennie is happily married to his wife, Betty, and they have four children: Michael, Glenn, Jennifer, and Cody, and six wonderful grandchildren: Dylan, Emily, Aniston, Trenton, McKinley, and Merritt.

Made in the USA
Coppell, TX
22 November 2024